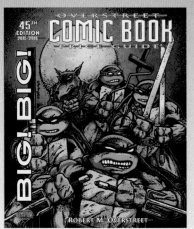

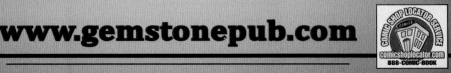

THE OVERSTREET® GUIDE TO COSPLAY

By Carrie Wood, Eddie Newsome & Melissa Bowersox

MARIANNE COLEMAN, KATIE FLEMING, MARK HUESMAN,
LIEBS COSPLAY, BRITANY MARRIOTT & J.C. VAUGHN
CONTRIBUTING WRITERS

MARK HUESMAN & CARRIE WOOD
LAYOUT & DESIGN

MARK HUESMAN
AMANDA SHERIFF
J.C. VAUGHN
EDITORS

GEMSTONE PUBLISHING • TIMONIUM, MARYLAND
WWW.GEMSTONEPUB.COM

Long before they called it "cosplay," there were enthusiasts who wanted to take their fandom to the proverbial next level and showed up at conventions wearing costumes of their favorite characters.

Casting the mind backward into earlier days, Trekkies (or Trekkers) were among the first real standouts. Superman was always a big one. Wendy Pini's turn as Red Sonja, accompanying artist Frank Thorne, was a great attention-getter. Looking back, there was perhaps more of it than we thought at the time.

But there was nothing that could have prepared us for the scope, impact and level of participation cosplay has today in the world of comic book conventions.

Have you seen how many Deadpools show up to greet creator Rob Liefeld? Have you met the many variations of Harley Quinn who line up for current writers Amanda Conner and Jimmy Palmiotti? Have you seen the Spider-Men who spend the money and join the queue for Stan Lee?

From Sailor Moon to Batman, from Thor to Pikachu, and from Klingons to Transformers, any large comic con – and many smaller ones – will have a serious contingent of cosplayers representing their favorite characters.

But who are they? What drives them? How can you become one of them?

Under the guidance of Gemstone's Carrie Wood, herself a veteran cosplayer, our team of authors, photographers and other contributors take on those questions and some of the key issues facing the world of cosplay.

If you're new to cosplay, thanks for making us an early stop on your journey. If you're already an informed enthusiast, we hope you'll think about things a bit differently after reading this book.

And if you're new to books from Gemstone Publishing, *The Overstreet Guide To Cosplay* is just the latest in our "how to" line. We hope you'll check out some of the others as well!

Sincerely,

Robert M. Overstreet
Publisher
feedback@gemstonepub.com

GEMSTONE PUBLISHING

STEPHEN A. GEPPI
PRESIDENT AND
CHIEF EXECUTIVE OFFICER

ROBERT M. OVERSTREET
PUBLISHER

J.C. VAUGHN
VICE-PRESIDENT
OF PUBLISHING

MARK HUESMAN
CREATIVE DIRECTOR

AMANDA SHERIFF
ASSOCIATE EDITOR

CARRIE WOOD
ASSISTANT EDITOR

BRAELYNN BOWERSOX
STAFF WRITER

WWW.GEMSTONEPUB.COM

GEPPI'S ENTERTAINMENT MUSEUM

STEPHEN A. GEPPI
FOUNDER AND
CHIEF EXECUTIVE OFFICER

MELISSA BOWERSOX
PRESIDENT

WWW.GEPPISMUSEUM.COM

Table of Contents

Table of Contents

Special Thanks to Richard Ankney, Archie Brown, Marianne Coleman, Kacie Doran, Jason Evans, Jerry Farmer, Katie Fleming, Veronica Fones, Tom Fulgione, Mary Grecco, Vikki Hughes, Jim Kuhoric, Tara Levin, Liebs Cosplay, Vira Mal, Britany Marriott, John W. McAdams III, Moana McAdams, Lauren McFadden, Ami Naugler, Jason Nieves, Jason Osborne, Jimmy Palmiotti, Mike Pfeffer, Allen Ryde, Wendell Smith, Michael Solof, J. Kevin Topham, Billy Tucci, Michael Wilson, Tiffany Witcher, Megan Zimmerman, ZippyC, and Tommy, Chris and Nick at Best Comics, ...and every cosplayer who stopped and smiled for a photo during the making of this book.

INTRODUCTION!

By Melissa Bowersox

It seems to me that what we now call cosplay has almost always been a part of my life.

My first experience with it was when I was six or seven years old; I was dressed up as Wonder Woman and took part in the kids' masquerade at a comic convention. I took second place. I got beat by Superman. I remember proudly posing just like Wonder Woman with my golden cuffs, which were made of felt.

After that first experience I had so many others simply because I was a kid who literally grew up in the comic industry. This rather unique perspective shows that even 30 years ago cosplay was a lot of fun, but that it wasn't anything out of the ordinary to me. One of the most memorable early times came when Darth Vader and Spider-Man accompanied my sister Danielle and me around Harborplace in Baltimore on the day it opened to the public.

My dad was opening his latest Geppi's Comic World location there that day. As he is, after all, Italian to the core, his overprotective nature meant he was terrified to let us walk around without a proper escort. We were the only kids with our own personal bodyguards, the aforementioned Darth Vader and Spidey.

As much as the people who saw my sister and me couldn't help but notice us and our more colorfully clad companions, for my part I couldn't help but be impressed with the costumes. That's an aspect that hasn't changed for me.

As an adult, what I find most impressive is not the actual costumes but the way you see so many cosplayers giving back to the community, whether it is cheering up a sick child or raising money for various charities. That generous spirit and giving nature is truly inspiring and in many instances represents the best of what we as fans and as an industry have to offer. There are so many cosplayers now at the average convention that it's difficult to remember what it was like before they were there.

But who are all of these cosplayers, and where did they come from? How did cosplay become such a part of the fabric of our industry? There was no single event or incident that made people start donning costumes and showing up at conventions and other events. Instead, the massive wave we now see has actually been building for years.

When I think about the early days, I can't help but think back to Wendy Pini as Red Sonja (frequently alongside Red Sonja artist Frank Thorne in a wizard costume) or original Star Trek fans in uniform at conventions. There were many costumes at science fiction conventions, some to a lesser extent at horror cons, and of course at comic book shows. By the time the 1980s rolled around, manga and anime conventions had begun to experience a real surge of cosplayers, and by the mid-1990s we saw a tremendous influx at Comic-Con International: San Diego when *Sailor Moon* went from big to huge.

None of that earlier growth prepared us for what we're seeing now: The beautifully executed intricate designs, the attention to detail, the inventive interpretation, the expressions of individuality, the team-ups, and of course the sheer number of cosplayers around. Even for those of us who have witnessed firsthand this explosion in popularity and in the effort required to make it happen, it's truly amazing!

What Carrie Wood, Eddie Newsome, our fellow contributors and I hope is that you'll find this book to be a thorough introduction to the world of cosplay and that, whether you're new to it or a seasoned pro, you'll come away from it with new inspiration.

Melissa Bowersox is the President of Geppi's Entertainment Museum.

Why Cosplay?

Why cosplay? It's one of the most difficult questions to give a definitive answer for, because every cosplayer has a unique experience and perspective. Everyone got started at a different point in their lives; for many, their reasons for starting and their reasons for continuing the hobby are different. While everyone has their own reason for putting on a wig and costume and parading around at a convention, it should be known – there's no wrong reason to cosplay!

For some, getting a chance to be someone else for a little while is enough.

"I think what really made me want to take part in cosplay was that you get to be someone different for a day," New York cosplayer Mary Grecco said. "Growing up, almost all of us wanted to be someone different, whether it be from a movie, anime, or a video game. We all had dreams to be a certain person. Picking a character and learning about them is the fun part. It's always fun having an alter ego."

Being able to not simply become the character, but to bring it to others, is the motivation behind many costumes, too. Jason Evans, from Baltimore, Maryland, said part of the reason he dons his costume is because cosplay adds a human element to the scene.

"I think that cosplay is the opportunity for your characters to come to life. You can look at comic books and watch movies, but if you see a living, breathing Superman or Batman or Hulk or anybody, I think that changes the entire dynamic of the whole convention," Evans said. "You can get toys and everything, but as a fan, for me, I think it's more of a human picture that you actually get to see someone as that character."

Evans, like many cosplayers, first got a taste of the costuming bug thanks to a certain holiday.

"At first, it was Halloween," he said. "I'd go out with a bunch of friends, and we'd dress up every year, and every year somebody would up the ante and somebody would have a better costume – it just grew from that. One year we decided to go to a comic convention, and it took off from there."

Seeing cosplay up-close and personal at conventions is what spurred many now-cosplayers into putting on a costume for the first time.

"My brother took me to Otakon in 2006, and after seeing so many amazing cosplayers, I was absolutely captivated," Maryland cosplayer Megan Zimmerman said. "I loved the transformation and the care that it took to become that character. It wasn't until a couple years later, when I entered high school, that I finally decided that I wanted to cosplay."

New York cosplayer Jason Nieves had already been going to conventions for years by the time he finally decided to cosplay.

"A few years back I started my own website, called The Nerd Truth, covering geek and nerd news in pop culture. Since I already attended many conventions, I decided to photograph and post from the cons, including, of course, cosplayers," Nieves said. "Meeting and even becoming friends with many of these cosplayers, I fell in love with this community of wonderful people. As a big fan of Halloween, and as a child who grew up dreaming of being a superhero, I was smitten with the idea of dressing up in character. But I was little embarrassed of my body shape. Eventually I gave in to the need to do this and jumped in! I haven't regretted it since."

So whether you're a newcomer to the convention scene or a seasoned attendee, a Halloween enthusiast or a superhero-in-training, it all goes to show – there's no wrong way to cosplay, and no wrong reason to get started.

ACCEPTANCE OF COSPLAY & HOW THE CULTURE HAS CHANGED

— By Eddie Newsome —

Until recently, wearing a mask, a cape, or even just a t-shirt showing your love of all things geek was taboo. It was the closest thing to a "kick me" or "un-dateable" sign you could wear, without someone actually coming up and putting one on you. But, somewhere along the line – maybe through television or movies, or a simple changing of the guard – people began to say, "Screw it! I paid for this Superman cape and by Crom I'm going to wear it to the comic book show!"

Cosplay has moved to the forefront of not just nerd culture, but pop culture in general. It has become a movement that has inspired creativity that people never knew they were capable of. It has moved hearts and souls to realize that they have kindred spirits, that they are not alone in their love and admiration of this culture.

Cosplay has become more than what it was at its conception. What was considered by many as simply "dress-up" has become a call to arms for individuality and self-ex-

pression. It's a culture that has many cheerleaders as well as detractors. Those who see cosplay as just a "new fad" that has limited staying power are diametrically opposed to the passion exhibited by those who see cosplay as the welcomed an embracing outlet for their love of all things geek. The opposition tends to come from a simple lack of understanding – why would anyone want to dress up from a comic book or a movie?

At the start of this hobby's rise to prominence, cosplay was looked down upon and thought of as just a kids-only activity. Now, it's ready for prime-time status. Cosplay has evolved and, like all forms of evolution, it mutates and grows stronger over time. Those who saw it as a fad are slowly coming to the realization that cosplay is more than just a passing fancy. It's a culture that is teaching acceptance, teamwork, and has crossed the divide of all genders, races, and other demographics.

Every day as the culture grows, so do those who are within the hobby, and in that comes a greater perspective. We who don the cape, mask or armor learn that there are more mediums out there in the world to reach out and connect with people. For those who don't understand cosplay – and there are some who don't and never will –

it's more than just people running around in spandex. Cosplay is crafting, planning, conception, hard work, and, for many of us, cosplay is also now a vastly social experience.

If you told me 20 years ago, "Eddie, don't worry! It's going to be cool to cosplay one day, and there will even be television shows about it soon," I would have slowly backed away and told you I need to check my two-way pager before running for the hills. But, lo and behold, society has evolved, and with the passing of time and the advent of new media, society has opened both arms and has given cosplay a big ol' grandma hug filled with love, appreciation and encouragement.

Societal changes in acceptance is directly correlated to what media embraces as "cool" and "hip." In the case of cosplay, it has filled the hearts and minds of old and young alike. From intricate costumes like Iron Man to Katniss from *The Hunger Games*, we see how even Hollywood has grown in its development. That growth came from those same people who, in their youth, sat creating and designing constantly. Thanks to popular cosplayers like YaYa Han, Ivy Doomkitty and Eric "The Smoke" Moran, cosplay has been given a home

online with tutorials, fan movies and more. The internet has become a place where we can see our face, talent and passion. It's given us a bridge to cross over and reach out to those who have a worldwide audience and connect with them.

But even with all this at our disposal, there is still an age barrier to be torn down. With shows like *Face/Off* and *Heroes of Cosplay*, we see behind the velvet rope of cosplay to the work and dedication it takes to bring fictional characters to life. The media has been both instrumental and detrimental to showing costume and prop-making as a skill and not just a hobby. With careful editing, we've seen heroes become villains and villains become misunderstood. But even with this, it's opened eyes and given more understanding to what we do and why we do it. As with many things, the path to great cosplay is set by those more experienced in real-world application of costuming, theatrics and other skills. This is then imitated by the fresh faces of the younger crowd that has grown up without the stigma of geek or nerd shame. Now, entire organizations, businesses and media channels have been born from the world of cosplay; with the adoption of new

media, the past barriers of geography and language have been broken down. And just as the torch is passed in other movements, so too must that of cosplay from the pro to the novice, from the old school to the new.

Once, the thought of dressing up in a costume to attend a convention was considered "weird" or "strange" by the masses, in the same way to how "geek" and "nerd" were not exactly terms of endearment. I personally experienced this – I was ridiculed as a kid growing up in Newark, NJ, because I would rather read a comic than do most other things. Rather than play basketball, I'd rather play X-Men. But where there used to be just two or three lonely nerds at the school lunch table with their comic books, there's now a huge group of kids – and it's not a "nerdy" thing to do anymore. Where there used to be a kid who watched TV and made costumes alone, there's now a weekend party host at a big convention. The words "geek" and "nerd" were once used to describe outsiders. Now, those terms are pretty hip – and I love it! I've gone from an African-American teen who felt awkward in his own skin, to a cosplayer who has been featured in newspapers and documentaries. It's been a long journey from sitting alone

at lunch and not even going to my own prom, to where I am now, and that's a beautiful thing by way of cosplay.

This is why I've taken up the cause of spreading acceptance and understanding in the cosplay community and in the general public. These are the dividends that are paid through diligence and acceptance of first who we are and then by the world.

One of the most beautiful things about cosplay is how it has been embraced worldwide and has connected and united people in a way that few other things can. For cosplayers, the hobby is the thread that unites us. Is there still a long way to go? Absolutely. But, we are closer than we were just five or 10 years ago. This journey of acceptance and inclusion has led the greater public to realize that cosplay is a lifestyle of passion and an outlet that has opened many doors for many different people. This is only the beginning.

TIPS AND TRICKS FOR CLOSET COSPLAY

By Carrie Wood

So you're heading to your next convention, and you want to participate as a cosplayer, but you don't have the skills to make your own costume, the time to order a mass-produced one from overseas, or the money to pay for a commission. Think you're out of options? Absolutely not!

There are plenty of character designs across comic books, video game, anime, television and more that can be very easily recreated just by diving through some old clothes, or by taking a quick trip to the thrift store. Even some of the most iconic looks in pop culture have been some of the simplest, so there's nothing holding you back from having a recognizable costume at a convention simply because you might not know how to operate a sewing machine.

Here are just a few ideas for when you need a costume on a time crunch:

Staple items

Unfortunately, what qualifies as a "staple item" – something simple that you can use for multiple outfits – differs a lot from person to person depending on what they're into. Someone who primarily cosplays from anime and manga might not require the same sort of staple items that someone who cosplays from comic books would need. That said, there are some things that are often used across the board.

Plain T-shirts can often be the basis for a solid closet costume. Sometimes taking an old shirt and adding a logo or a design by simply painting it on can instantly make you recognizable as the character. Heading to your local thrift store can also lead to some great finds, like a good leather jacket (is there a series that *doesn't* feature someone in leather?) or some outlandish boots.

Most superheroes aren't in their day-saving outfits all the time, so finding their "secret identity" outfits can be pretty easy just by going through the racks at a department store. For some other outfits that are consistently seen across multiple series – such as school outfits in anime and manga – picking up common items like pleated skirts and a sailor-cuffed top can be applied to multiple characters. I've put together costumes out of my closet just by matching different items with the same blue pleated skirt I've had for years!

People who are interested in cosplaying female characters should definitely keep some items consistently on-hand in order to quickly throw together an outfit. Hosiery – particularly different-colored dance tights – and swimsuits can be the first steps towards a superhero outfit. I personally recommend dance tights because of how thick they are compared to department store hosiery, meaning their color is opaque from top to bottom and doesn't fade when it stretches, and they also tend to develop

runs less often. Swimsuits can be a great basis for a closet outfit, particularly plain, solid-colored one-piece suits. I saw a girl once put together a perfect Black Canary outfit with a black swimsuit, cheap fishnets, and a black leather jacket she found at a thrift store.

Basically, if you know the kinds of characters you want to portray, and you've got some time and extra cash to raid your thrift store, you can come up with some solid items that can be used again and again across different characters and even different series.

Business wear is your friend

To go off of the last point, sometimes simply owning a decent suit can mean you have the ability to be a number of different characters. Plenty of heroes wear their costumes under their business clothes, too – do you have a Superman shirt, glasses and a good suit? Congratulations, you're now Clark Kent! Unbutton the dress shirt to reveal the Superman logo underneath and recreate one of the most classic poses in comics. Characters from Spider-Man to Captain America and even the Green Lantern have all participated in this trope, and shirts can easily be found that replicate their costumes, so don your best suit and tie and be the hero you were meant to be!

Hair and makeup can be the focus...

If you (or someone you know) has any sort of skill with costume or stage-quality makeup, it almost doesn't matter

what you've got on! There have been a number of characters with some unique skin tones over the years, and stage make-up has been easier than ever to find thanks to the marvels of technology. So if this ends up being your fancy, rather than building armor or sewing costumes, you can start to base "closet" outfits off of it. These sort of characters also tend to be recognizable no matter what they've got on; if you're painted blue and have a tail, people will see you as Nightcrawler even if you end up wearing, say, a Hawaiian shirt and sandals. Zombie makeup has also become super popular at conventions with the continued popularity of zombie-centric series, so getting a little gray and bloody (and maybe tearing up some old clothes you weren't going to wear again anyway) can turn into a costume on its own. Getting creative with makeup

opens up more doors for cosplay than many other techniques!

This probably applies more to anime and manga than it does anything else, but having a good wig can also lend itself to not needing to spend much time on the actual costume itself. If you discover a talent for hair styling, that can easily be the centerpiece of an outfit. There are some classic anime hairstyles that are automatically recognizable as the character regardless of what ends up being worn with it – Goku (from *Dragon Ball*) and Sailor Moon both apply here. If you can nail the ridiculous hairstyle, you almost don't need to do anything else.

...But so can a good prop

A good prop doesn't have to be a big one – just a recognizable one. Plenty of popular characters wear plain clothes, but having a signature item can make your outfit stand out that much more. We've got just a couple of examples here, but it applies to just about any character that's had a signature item over the years.

Most of the Doctors from *Doctor Who* have worn outfits that are fairly reasonable in terms of recreating them out of a thrift store, but having the appropriate Sonic Screwdriver will make the costume. It's easy to fashion a green tunic out of a big shirt to create Link's outfit from *The Legend of Zelda*, but having the Master Sword will

make you stand out.

Iron Man might be a difficult project, but his alter-ego is just as recognizable thanks to the film series. It's easy to buy a cheap plastic replica of an arc reactor that will actually light up, so by sticking that under a black t-shirt and growing out your goatee, well, congratulations, you're now a billionaire playboy philanthropist. For his fellow Avenger, Thor, all you really need to do is have blonde hair and Mjolnir; he's had a number of more casual outfits outside of his Asgardian armor, but as long as you hold that hammer, people will know who you are.

Understand the scope of your project

This applies to just about any costume, but it should be stated again here. Even if you need to go to the store and buy pieces to turn into an outfit, you need to give yourself enough time to do that. There's always the chance that even if you hit every thrift store in your area, you just won't find a jacket that will work for your outfit. Even if it's a costume that can be put together

entirely from simple things at a department store, the more complicated a costume is – the more pieces it has – the more difficult it will be to complete because of the higher amount of things that can simply go wrong.

As with all of our cosplay advice in this book, it's important to keep in mind that no matter what, the number-one priority should be to have fun. Whether you're in your regular business clothes as Clark Kent or if you spent weeks building armor, as long as you have a good time, you're being a good cosplayer. "Closet Cosplay" is not something to be looked down upon; it is great for the beginner, the casual cosplayer, or for the veteran who wants a last-minute addition – just enjoy the hobby for what it is and embrace your character in your own way!

WHAT TO EXPECT WHEN BUYING YOUR COSPLAY

By Carrie Wood

As cosplay has become increasingly popular, the business of selling costumes and related items has also grown exponentially. Outfits of popular characters from anime, video games and comic books are now mass produced around the world and can easily be purchased online. For those who maybe lack sewing skills, buying a costume can often seem like the easiest, fastest, and most cost-effective way to cosplay their favorite character.

Though purchasing a costume can now be as simple as typing a few words into Google and seeing what comes up, it hasn't always been that way. When I first started cosplaying in the early 2000s, it was next to impossible to find anything cosplay-related online. These days, it's super easy to find costumes from just about every series. I've purchased props, parts of costumes and even entire ensembles from online sellers before, and for the most part, my experience has been pretty good. I haven't had an experience completely turn me off from the idea of just clicking the "Buy" button to get a costume, and I consider it a worthwhile alternative to making a costume, especially if you lack the sewing skills to make something on your own. I've sewn my own outfits for years and for some things it's just a lot easier to buy it than it is to make it.

As, admittedly, my own mass-produced

Buying a costume means that everyone in a group can match perfectly without much effort. With the rise in popularity of sports-themed anime, bought costumes have also been seen more often.

costume experience is somewhat limited, I sought out other cosplayers who have their own experiences to share. Over the course of these conversations, many of my own ideas about purchasing a mass-made costume were confirmed, though others were dispelled.

What I did notice about most of the people I spoke with about these sort of purchas-

Veronica Fones, seen above, bought her biking uniform. Though it's clear the outfit photographs well, Fones said that because of the fact that cheap, low-quality polyester tends to be used for these mass-produced outfits, it can be annoying for cosplayers who want something sturdier or a little more show-accurate.

"All the costumes I've bought have been a fairly decent quality for the amount of money I paid for them, although costumes bought in 2014 and 2015 have been of a much higher quality and also had more sizes available than the one I bought in 2009," she said. "In general I think it's a lot less stressful to buy instead of make a costume, because it's just one step – buying – versus getting materials and trying to meet a deadline."

However, there's plenty more than just sports jerseys available. Tom "Bearpigman" Fulgione has purchased multiple different outfits from online cosplay retailers over the last several years, including a three-piece suit in a pretty unusual color (lime green), a Japanese-style high school boys' uniform, and a formal butler's coat with accessories. His experience with the green suit in particular left him with some pretty strong opinions on the idea of buying a costume.

"Before I made the purchase, I was pretty hesitant about it," he said. "For the price of the suit alone, I could have made a ton of smaller, cheaper cosplays, but that color was very difficult and I didn't know anyone with the skills to make a suit from scratch. I was pretty unhappy with the product they sent me. It was pretty ill-fitting – even after taking proper measurements – and required some extra tailoring before I could wear it. Even then, it was snug, and I always feared that it would tear, as the material it was made out of was pretty thin and flimsy."

Tom summed up his cosplay buying experience with the eternal phrase: "You get what you pay for."

"If it's a casual outfit, or something generic-looking, or something that I'm not super invested in, I'll consider buying a mass-produced outfit rather than waste time trying to make it," he said. "But if it's a cosplay I really care about, then for sure I'm going to spend the extra money and commission the costume from a friend who knows more about sewing, fabric choices, and making better-fitting clothing for me than someone overseas."

The one very important sticking point with these costumes that was almost universally agreed upon with these cosplayers is that it's incredibly important to pay attention to the sizing chart – and even then, maybe try and give yourself a little extra breathing room.

"You usually will have to alter a bought costume in some way, because they aren't

es is that you might not always get exactly what you paid for.

"One of the factors I've come to expect from mass-produced costumes is the material to be misrepresented in the descriptions," cosplayer Veronica Fones said. "Jerseys from different sports anime are almost always a cheap polyester material, despite the posted descriptions. The fabric photographs well, so it's not really a huge problem, but when going for exact accuracy it isn't right, which is annoying as a buyer."

With the incredible popularity of different sports-themed anime such as *Yowamushi Pedal*, *Haikyuu!*, *Free! Iwatobi Swim Club*, and *Kuroko's Basketball*, mass-produced uniforms have become a common sight at many different anime conventions. Cosplayer Ami Naugler has bought these sort of uniforms multiple times, and has noticed a trend in the mass-produced costume industry.

Pfeffer said. "It was remarkably well made; the stitching was tight and seams weren't visible. It was unlined, had no belt loops in the pants or any other devices to finely adjust the fit… [but] it fit darn near perfectly. It had several layers – shirt, vest, jacket – but it was easy to move in. It had a couple of decorative bows that needed pinning on, but that wasn't too troublesome."

The final point that must be made about mass-produced costumes is that it's important to give yourself enough time for the outfit to arrive. Since most of these companies are located in Asia, for someone in North America, it can take several weeks for the package to arrive. Buying a costume is not something that can be done last-minute before a convention (at least not without paying exorbitant shipping fees). Everyone I spoke with said that it took anywhere from four to eight weeks for their item to arrive.

being made to your exact specifications," Ami said. "There's usually a few hanging threads that will have to be removed, and a lot of the time at least one piece will have to be hemmed as well."

In my own buying experience, I tend to buy a size or two up if I'm not confident in the sizing chart being accurate, since it's easy to have something taken in than dealing with a too-snug costume. It helps that I have sewing skills myself, so that I can make these adjustments easy, but even for someone without a sewing machine, it's pretty easy to find someone else with a machine who can bring a too-big garment in a few inches. However, cosplayer Mike Pfeffer bought an anime outfit online and had an overall very positive experience with the sizing, despite other hiccups with the outfit.

"The ordering process included details on how to spec it out, where the measurements should be taken, and how to take them accurately. I needed another person to hold the measuring tape but that was the hardest part,"

Ultimately, buying your costume can be a worthwhile cosplay investment if you lack the ability to make it yourself, or if you want to take that time to focus on other projects. There are plenty of retailers online that sell costumes from a seemingly infinite amount of series; they can be found on websites such as eBay or Etsy, but sometimes spending a few minutes in a search engine can also produce good results. There are pros and cons to this approach to cosplay, as there are with every approach, so if you're looking to buy your next costume, keep these cosplayers' opinions and experiences in mind before hitting that "Buy" button.

A bought costume straight out of the package:

The uniform seen here was purchased from an online seller in early 2015. As you can see to the right, there's some unfinished and slightly fraying edges on the inside. Not a huge deal though, since you can trim that stuff up easily - and it's not as though anyone's going to see the inside of your costume!

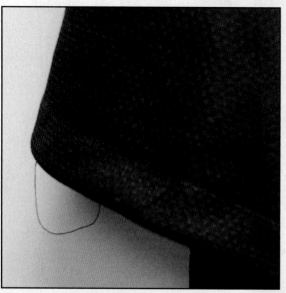

The two big beefs that I had with this outfit were the quality of material and the amount of strings that could be seen hanging off from nearly every stitch. You can see one of them to the left - there were probably a dozen in total, and it was a little annoying to have to go through and snip everything off. It's hard to tell by the photo, but the material just feels cheap and low-quality. It's definitely not the level of material that you would expect out of even a generic sports uniform.

I also did order this a size up than what I would normally wear. It fit me perfectly out of the bag, just confirming that in a lot of cases, these sort of uniforms tend to run a little small. The upsides are many, though: I get a nice-looking costume for a fraction of the time and material cost if I tried to make it myself, I perfectly match all of my cosplayer friends who are also cosplaying from this series, and despite some loose strings and frayed edges, it's of a decent enough quality that I'll probably buy again.

COMMISSIONING TIPS FOR A POSITIVE COSPLAY EXPERIENCE

By Carrie Wood

Cosplay commissions can encompass every aspect of an outfit – the costume itself, props, wigs, accessories, and more. Even those who have been cosplaying for years often commission parts of a costume from someone else, so don't think that asking for help on a costume or having someone else make the whole thing is by any means a bad thing. Someone who's great at sewing might not be so good at wigs, and someone who can make armor might not be able to put together a pair of pants. There's a wealth of different talents in the cosplay community, and being able to share those talents with others is what makes the process of commissioning so great.

I've been on both sides of the commission equation – I've made costumes for friends, but I've also commissioned a number of different people for props, wigs, and even entire costumes. Here are my top pieces of advice for anyone looking to either commission a costume, as well as for anyone looking to start making cosplays for others.

Create a contract and set appropriate deadlines

It's surprising that this isn't more obvious or widely done, but for some reason, contracts haven't been a trend when it comes to commissioning cosplay items.

But it's absolutely necessary, for a number of reasons; it sets up an agreement for the most crucial things about a commissioned outfit – the cost per hour of labor, and the timeline by which progress should be made. This helps hold both the customer, and the person they're commissioning from, more accountable than if no formal agreement is agreed upon.

Create a payment plan that works for both parties

This is the sort of thing that should be topic number one when laying out plans for a commissioned costume. There are a few ways to go about it, and each may work well for different people in different situations.

Lump sums up front can be risky for both parties. The upside for this is the person working gets their payment all at once, and the person paying can relax knowing that they won't be billed for anything else in the future. There are plenty of down-

sides, however. The biggest might come from either party miscalculating the amount of time and effort that it would take to produce the piece – leading to either the person making the piece being frustrated with too little funding for the amount of time, or the person receiving the item ending up peeved with perhaps overpaying for something that didn't reach expectations.

Lump sums at the end can also carry issues, though there's less risks involved. The upside is that the person who completed the work knows exactly how much effort went into it at the end of the project and can bill the customer appropriately. Plus, the customer can determine if this is a fair price or not upon seeing a completed item. The biggest downside to this method is that workers have ended up with dissatisfied customers that don't pay up for the item upon completion, leaving the worker with lots of hours logged and no paycheck at the end of the day.

Paying all at once is generally best for

Photographs provided by Allen Ryde

smaller, less costly projects than large, expensive and elaborate ones. For customers in particular, lump sums of several hundred dollars for a big prop or outfit can also be difficult to manage – and for that reason, a spaced-out payment plan is recommended for bigger projects.

This is something that should be hashed out in the aforementioned contract, but when creating a payment plan, lay it out so that payments should be made as progress is also made. Having payments match deadlines on certain aspects of a project not only makes sense, but it then incentivizes the person working on the project to make sure it gets done by that date. Many seamstresses and propmakers have taken to asking for a standard deposit up front to help pay for the initial cost of materials and the first bit of labor, and then charging the rest of the labor costs in chunks as the project is completed. This process allows flexibility on both ends, as the worker is able to be paid essentially as things are done, and the customer can then pay in several smaller chunks rather than as one big sum at the start or end of the project.

When it comes to actually paying, also be sure to use a method that can provide a receipt for both parties, such as a check or a PayPal transaction. If cash is the only option, make sure a receipt is written up with one of those old-fashioned carbon-paper receipt pads or something similar – so that both parties have a slip that can say "This amount was paid on this date and this is the balance remaining." This plays into our next point, which is…

Hold on to receipts and track your work

For seamstresses and prop-makers, this is essential for having a trusting relationship with your customer. When a customer is able to see what specifically their money went to, they will be more likely to come back to you in the future – it's pretty simple! Whenever something is bought for the costume, be sure to hold the receipt in a safe place. Creating a spreadsheet or something similar to keep track of how

many hours you've put into the costume is also good to do, so that you can accurately charge for labor rather than over- or under-charging your customer.

Value your work (and time) appropriately

Dear seamstresses, prop-makers, stylists, and other cosplay-related workers: don't undervalue yourself! These abilities are trained skills that not that many people have, and there's nothing more important than valuing these skills appropriately. Charging labor by the hour is a pretty standard practice for commissions, so be sure to set a rate that you feel is right for your skills and experience (hint: it should be a lot more than minimum wage!) If someone commissioning you for an outfit, wig, accessory or whatever else tells you that you rates are too costly, don't be afraid to put your foot down. Learning to sew, sculpt, or do any other craft takes time and effort – so getting a proper return on that investment is only fair.

For those looking to commission someone for an outfit: keep the above paragraph in mind. Sewing is significantly more involved than what you may have learned in your middle school home economics class, and making a costume involves application of a skill that has been developed over likely many years. Knowing this beforehand and respecting this ability will lead to a mutually beneficial and positive relationship between you and the person working on the project.

Know your limits

This goes for both the person working on the project and the customer. For the customer, this has more to do with a financial limit. Don't expect a big elaborate costume to be a budget project. Know how much you're willing to spend on something before you decide to begin a project; the previously discussed extended payment plan, where payments are made over the course of a project, often helps alleviate some budgetary issues.

For the people working on the project – don't take on anything that's beyond your ability! That's not to say that challenging projects should be avoided at all costs. It is simply important to know what your strengths and weaknesses are, and not to bite off more than you can chew. If you've never made anything skin-tight before, and someone wants a Catwoman suit, maybe think twice before taking on that project. If someone is looking for a gown and you tend to focus more on molded prop and armor work, maybe pass that project on to someone else.

This also applies to knowing how much time it takes for you to make something, and how much time you're being given for the project. If you're a full-time student or you have another job, it's going to be significantly tougher on you to pump out an outfit in a few weeks than it is for someone who uses costume-making as their primary source of income. And if the person asking for the outfit absolutely *needs* for it to be done quickly, charge a rush order. If you're going to stress yourself out and lose sleep over the making of an outfit for someone else, don't be afraid to charge extra per hour for those labor hours. I know my sleep time is precious to me – if I'm losing it to make an outfit for someone else, that person should be expected to pay for the rush order.

One of the best things about the cosplay community is how close-knit it tends to be. If someone can't make a big prop sword, chances are they know someone who can. While the dollar signs are often tempting, the damage to someone's reputation when they start a project and are unable to complete it satisfactorily (or at all!) can hurt way worse than a missed paycheck. There's no shame in saying "Hey, this is out of my skill set – but here's someone else you can talk to about this sort of thing instead!"

If possible, get fitted!

This really only applies to costumes, but it's so important that it needed to be included in this list. From the time a project is started to the time it's near completion, a change in weight or measurements is entirely possible. While a fitting might not be possible, depending on how far apart both parties are, if it is possible, it should absolutely be done. A fitting of a garment as it's in mid-completion can spare customers from headaches and disappointment. If a fitting cannot be done, the customer should definitely make any note of any significant weight changes so that the seamstress can make the appropriate changes before completion of the costume.

Photograph provided by Jerry Farmer

Show your progress

Few things can be as nerve-wracking for a customer as paying hundreds of dollars for a costume or prop and then not getting even so much as a peek at it until it's been delivered. As stages of progress are made, the person working on the item should do their absolute best to provide photos of it to their customer. This way, the customer can provide feedback during the construction process so that the person doing the work can make adjustments before the item is completed, and will ultimately result in greater satisfaction (and less frustration) for both parties.

Be professional

While most people who make costumes or props for other people are doing it as a side-business for some extra income, rather than as a full-time job or career, maintaining a professional attitude is one of the most important things you can do. If something goes wrong during the construction process, or if a customer is unsatisfied with the end result, complaining about how someone didn't like your work on social media is the worst thing you can possibly do for your business. Nothing says "unprofessional" like someone who doesn't know how to handle criticism. Rather than sulking or getting angry about it in public, have a conversation with your customer as to why they're unsatisfied, and do what you can to try and rectify the situation. Sometimes an unsatisfied customer will never be happy with what you do – and that sucks, but there's nothing you can do about it, and lashing out at negative comments on social media will ultimately make everything worse.

Having a professional attitude is also something that the customer should try and do. If the item you ordered comes in and you're not totally happy with it, rather than using that opportunity to immediately bash the person who worked on it, instead, try and work something out. If you ordered a jacket and it's too loose, see if you can have it taken in. If you get a prop and the paint is already starting to chip, see if it can be re-painted and sealed properly. With many cosplay problems, there's often a simple fix for it. Ultimately, try to be as constructive with your criticism as possible, rather than raging online about it.

That about wraps it up! While there's plenty of details in any individual project that would have to be hashed out on a case-by-case basis, the advice above can apply to really any commission. Whether you're about to order your first costume or you're making your 50th prop for someone else, these are some tips to keep in mind for a happy and positive customer relationship and a successful business.

Photograph provided by Jerry Farmer

Cosplayer Spotlight: Carrie Wood

Photo credit:
Richard Ankney

Describe your introduction to cosplay.
Carrie Wood (CW): My first convention was Otakon 2002, which is just an enormous convention to start with. Even then it was filling the Baltimore Convention Center. I was 12 years old, really getting into anime for the first time, and my friend and her parents brought me along. And everywhere I looked, there was someone else in cosplay. I still have a couple of photos of me at that convention, standing very awkwardly next to some *Trigun* cosplayers.

But that sudden overexposure to it all at once was what got me interested. Everyone in costume sort of seemed like they were having more fun than everyone not in costume, so I wanted to join in.

What is it about cosplay that makes you want to participate in the hobby?

CW: That's hard to describe, and I think it's different for everybody. Ultimately, I think I do it because I have a passion for the character or the series, and because I like to have a creative outlet to express that passion. Some people who are really into a show write fan fiction or create gorgeous works of fan art based off of it.

I'm not great at either of those things, but I think I'm competent enough with sewing at this point to pay tribute to a series through recreating my favorite character myself!

Have you ever met the creators/artists/writers of the characters you cosplay?

CW: I have! The creator of the *Touhou Project* series of games, ZUN, was at Anime Weekend Atlanta in 2013. I was dressed as the main playable character from the series, Reimu, and I ran into him and his wife outside of the hotel where the convention was taking place. I was a little nervous to speak to him, since I didn't want to intrude, but his wife saw me first and pointed me out to ZUN.

He came right over, just saying, "Oh!! Reimu! Great Reimu! Wow!" over and over. His wife took a picture of us together. I was beaming the rest of the weekend.

Do you make your own costumes? How?

CW: I do, for the most part. Sometimes I enlist help from some friends of mine who are way more talented than I am — I have a close friend who went to college with me, but his major was costume design. He's been a huge resource for me in the past, and I'm glad that I'm friends with someone so talented and willing to help.

But generally I try to find a pattern to adapt and then wing it the rest of the way. I made my Captain Marvel outfit off of one of those onesie pajama patterns! Almost everything I've made on my own has been tweaked from an existing pattern.

FABRIC CHOICES

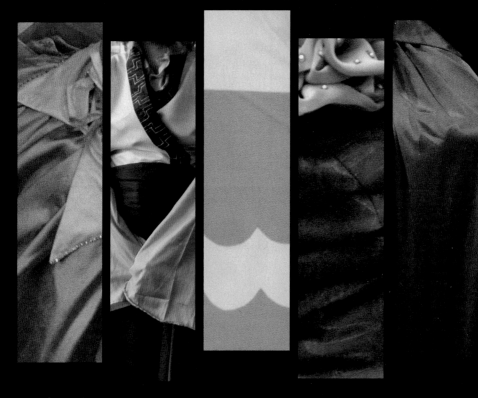

Before sitting down to make a costume yourself, it's important to plan out your approach to your project. While every costume is different, one of the most crucial decisions in every outfit is what fabric to use. Choosing the wrong fabric can make your costume look, well, wrong! And as any trip to the craft store can prove, there are so many different materials to choose from that it can become overwhelming to an inexperienced seamstress very quickly.

To give the fullest view of the wide world of fabrics we spoke with four different cosplayers of varying experience levels. We hope that their shared experience can provide you with a better eye for your next cosplay project!

Lauren McFadden
VintageAerith

How long have you been making your own outfits?

Lauren McFadden (LM): I've been making my own outfits since 2009, when a good friend on my dorm floor in college helped me learn to use a sewing machine. She assisted heavily throughout my first handmade costume attempt, and after that, I launched forward into making everything on my own.

What are your favorite fabrics to work with? Why?

LM: My absolute favorite fabric to work with is milliskin spandex. It's super-forgiving, doesn't ever fray, and gives a gorgeous flawless matte appearance. It has a beautiful drape, too! Out of the woven fabric family, I think twill is my favorite. It has just a slight bit of stretch, and makes for crisp, flat garments. The most important thing to me in cosplay is to create garments that don't fold or wrinkle anywhere that it can be avoided, to give a more cartoon- or game-like appearance.

Photo: @WardStradlater

How about least favorite?

LM: Satin is probably the fabric I hate the most. No matter how cleanly you cut your pieces or sew it together, it always manages to catch and reflect light the wrong way and makes a perfectly acceptable fit look wrinkly and incorrect. I try to use a matte satin or the reverse side of it whenever I can. Also, I avoid broadcloth as much as possible, unless a historical costume calls for a plain cotton.

Are there any fabrics you would say are universally good for most costume situations?

LM: If you can, try to shop in the twills, shirtings, and bottomweights. They

don't fray too badly, come in a wide variety of colors, and can usually be crisp *or* drape-y, depending on what you're looking for! Avoid shiny fabrics unless they have a "matte" shine... my rule is, buy fabric for the lowest common denominator of camera that might capture your costume. A dark photo with a bright flash will make shiny fabric look lurid and over-the-top.

What would you say is the most important thing to keep in mind when picking out fabric?

LM: The most important thing in choosing fabric, more so than the correct texture, is to remember color relativity. If it's hard to find the exact shade of color you need, and you are forced to go with an alternative, make sure

Photo: Sorairo-Days Photography

every other fabric you choose relates to *that* color--not the unobtainable "correct" one. It won't do any good to have a costume that has half the correct colors and half wildly incorrect ones... make sure they all relate to *each other*, even if the first one you chose isn't dead-accurate. As an example, one time I needed to create a costume out of only black and a vivid kelly green. One of the fabrics needed to be sheer chiffon with stripes of solid green. When I found the absolute perfect fabric in a store in New York City, I made the executive decision that I would base every green in the costume off the one in the striped chiffon, even though it was more of a dark forest green than a vivid kelly green. The unification of the colors paid off and the costume looked really great, whereas a mix of correct and incorrect greens would have looked strange.

Photo: Rene Hwang Photography

The other most important thing to keep in mind: try not to settle! If that color or texture isn't exactly perfect, don't spring for it. You might get lucky looking somewhere else!

Do you have any big fabric successes (or regrets) when it comes to your costumes?
LM: Quick story: when I was very new to cosplay, I spent hours picking the perfect fabrics for one of my first costumes. I chose a beautiful matte crepe pink that I thought would photograph really nice and flat. A day or two later when I dug into my shopping bag to begin, I took a quick glance at the fabric and went "oh, okay, here's the good side and here's the reverse side" - shiny satin versus matte satin. I trusted the amount of time I had agonized over which fabric to get, but when the costume was complete, I was super unhappy... why? I had totally bought that fabric while looking at its reverse side--it had been wound onto the bolt *backwards* at the fabric store. As a newbie to cosplay, I didn't know that it's perfectly acceptable to put the "shiny" side on the inside, and probably would've liked the costume way

better if I'd used the "wrong" side for the body of the costume. Moral of the story is, with fabric, there are no rules! Use the side of the fabric you like better!

Vira Mal

How long have you been making your own outfits?
Vira Mal (VM): I made my first costume in 2009, but I didn't really get into cosplay until mid-2012, so let's say... a bit over three years?

What are your favorite fabrics to work with? Why?
VM: I love wool blend suitings! It's easy to sew and iron, and the finished garment hangs nicely on your body.

I'm also a fan of casa/duchess satin, but this might be because of my love for giant dresses. It irons and sews pretty well, and the final result has a more subtle sheen to it than other types of satin. My third costume ever was made of five yards of casa satin, so I think it's not too bad for a beginner to work with.

I've also been very into sewing spandex and lycra recently. I used to hate working with them until I learned that the secret to sewing super stretchy knits is a walking foot. That foot is a life saver. I can even do embroidery on lycra with it!

How about least favorite?

VM: Anything that's cheap, unnaturally stiff, and wrinkles easily! (I'm looking at you, Symphony broadcloth.) Even if your craftsmanship skills are up to par, sometimes you just can't get the material to sit right or iron out well. It just adds an unnecessary level of difficulty to your work.

I'm also not a fan of faux fur due to the sheer amount of fur I get everywhere. So much sneezing.

Are there any fabrics you would say are universally good for most costume situations?

VM: Cotton sateen and softer twills probably have you covered for many, many outfits. I've started buying white cotton sateen and black stretch twill by the bolt since I'm using them so often. If you don't know where to start, wander in the bottomweights section of your local fabric store and you'll be fine 75 percent of the time.

What would you say is the most important thing to keep in mind when picking out fabric?

VM: Drape and weight are equally important! Let's take a pleated skirt for example. We'd want a material that's relatively heavy and stiff.

Now let's look at some materials that only satisfy one of these qualities. A heavy knit might have a good weight, but it lacks the stiffness to take a pleat. Organza might be stiff, but it's too light for a skirt. Both of these materials are terrible choices, so we need to keep both drape and weight in mind.

I like to scrunch up a bit of the fabric in my hand for about 15 seconds to see how it feels. It also acts as a wrinkle test!

Any other fabric advice you'd like to share?

VM: Don't buy fabric for a costume when you're brand spanking new at garment sewing and then finally get around to making the costume two years later. You'll wonder what the hell you were thinking when you look at the fabric you bought.

Zippy C

How long have you been making your own outfits?

Zippy C (ZC): I've been cosplaying since 2002! I started sewing a little before then, but I've been sewing seriously for 13 years.

What are your favorite fabrics to work with? Why?

ZC: Cotton sateen! It rips easily, irons crisp, and is great for a lot of garments. It has a bit of stretch to it so it's more versatile than normal cotton. It's also easy to find in a ton of colors. I also use gabardine a lot; it's great for suits and dress slacks when wool suiting isn't practical, and is easier to find odd colors in.

How about least favorite?

ZC: Silk charmeuse; it has a great drape but cutting it is a literal nightmare. It's very slippery and stretches out when you iron it which is a pain because it messes up your grainlines. Long pile fur is a general horror to work with, it sheds everywhere and can clog up machines.

Are there any fabrics you would say are universally good for most costume situations?

ZC: Kona Cotton is good mid-weight fabric for a lot of costumes, and cotton twill is a nice basic bottomweight fabric for thicker garments like jackets. Casa Satin works nicely for costumes that need a little more flow or sheen.

What would you say is the most important thing to keep in mind when picking out fabric?

ZC: Picking out a fabric that's appropriate for the garment you're trying to make! Like dress shirts are generally made from cotton or cotton/poly blends, et cetera. If the character has high resolution references where you can tell the weave of the fabric trying to match, that is helpful, or if the costume is historical, checking the types of fabrics used in that era is also smart. If I have to choose between exact color accuracy and perfect fabric type for a costume, I'll always go with the fabric type.

Do you have any big fabric successes (or regrets) when it comes to your costumes?

ZC: Finding the loveliest purple peachskin in the garment district and buying the whole bolt was a success for me and a regret for my wallet.

Also don't use expensive Chinese plush silk velvet for a cape that might risk dragging across a carpet. Do not do it.

Tara Levin

How long have you been making your own outfits?

Tara Levin (TL): The first costume I made entirely by myself was Miroku from InuYasha in 2003, so 12 years. The two before that were largely thanks to the very limited patience and sewing knowledge of my mother.

What are your favorite fabrics to work with? Why?

TL: Sateen is my absolute favorite. Many costumes, especially those from animated media, tend to have large blocks of solid color, and sateen has such a lovely subtle shine to it that really lends itself well to cosplay. It's also slightly stretchy (good for not-quite-exact measurements) and is of a decent weight so as to be heavy enough to drape well and be opaque but not too heavy so as to be uncomfortable. Finally, it comes in tons of colors, and even if you can't find just the right shade, it's easily dyeable.

I also really like working with vinyl, because I hate myself I guess! But seriously, the challenge of making 3D objects like pouches out of vinyl has always been fun for me.

How about least favorite?

TL: As a former colorguard girl, I still have nightmares about crushed velvet. It feels gross, it looks gross, and it's always uncomfortably heavy. I don't understand why it exists. Also, for the love of all that is good, please leave the costume satin section be.

Are there any fabrics you would say are universally good for most costume situations?

TL: I cannot recommend sateen enough for most situations! As a medium-weight fabric it is super useful in many weather situations and for many different clothing types, and with its minor amount of stretch, it is quite forgiving! Additionally, if you're looking for a stiffer fabric for something

All photos provided by Tara Levin

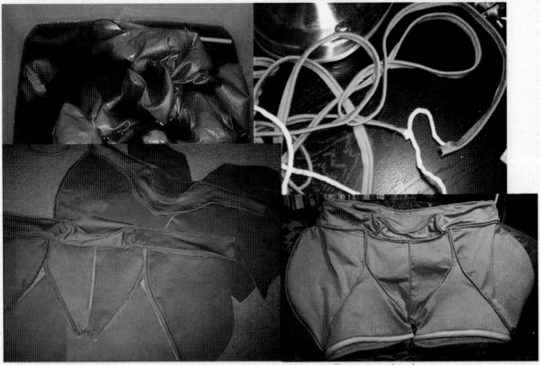

Dyeing the shorts fabric

Hand-made piping (almost 12 yards)

Shorts in pieces

Shorts completed

like a military or school uniform but are worried about it being too hot and heavy, I really like twill.

What would you say is the most important thing to keep in mind when picking out fabric?
TL: While there's a lot to consider in regards to picking out fabric – price, matching color, drape, stretch vs. non-stretch, ironability, etc. – for me, the most important thing is comfort. If you're uncomfortable in a costume because you picked a fabric too heavy (or too light) for the weather, or if it's too sheer, or too stiff, you're not going to want to wear that costume for very long. And that's unfortunate, because more than likely you've put a ton of effort into that costume, and you should be able to enjoy it as much as possible!

Do you have any big fabric successes (or regrets) when it comes to your costumes?
TL: One year for a winter con, I made a genderbent version of North from *Rise of the Guardians*, and was determined to make her iconic coat out of the best possible materials, regardless of price. I had

the option of using either real wool or synthetic wool, and while the former was tempting, I was glad I ended up with the synthetic. It was still warm but breathed much better, making it more comfortable inside the convention center. It was also much easier to work with and handled washing and general wear better than real wool would have.

A couple years previous at the same con, I endured a massive undertaking when I decided to painstakingly piece together the shorts for Dragon Kid from *Tiger & Bunny* by hand – complete with over 11 yards of hand-made piping. This was a massive undertaking, and I don't know how I would have managed it on a less forgiving fabric than sateen. Not only could I dye it closer to the color I wanted, but the stretch of the fabric made both making and applying the piping less miserable than it could have been. (It won the weekend in Hall Cosplay that year, too, so I really cannot recommend this stuff enough!)

On the flip-side... Mamas, don't let your babies make kimono out of costume satin to wear in the summer Baltimore heat. Trust me.

SEWING MACHINE THREAD TENSION

by Marianne Coleman (http://www.facebook.com/mazcostuts)

A significant number of the frustrations associated with using a sewing machine, such as snapped thread, broken needles, bird nest of thread in the feed dogs, and bunched up fabric, can be caused by incorrect tension settings on the machine. Most tension issues originate from the top thread – it's rare to need to adjust your bobbin tension. This tutorial will demonstrate how to determine the correct top thread tension for the fabric you're sewing, using a spare scrap of fabric.

Step 1: Set your machine to straight stitch and the longest stitch setting. This is known as a basting stitch. Thread up your machine with a different colour on the top and bottom thread. This is to help you understand the relationship between too much tension and not enough.

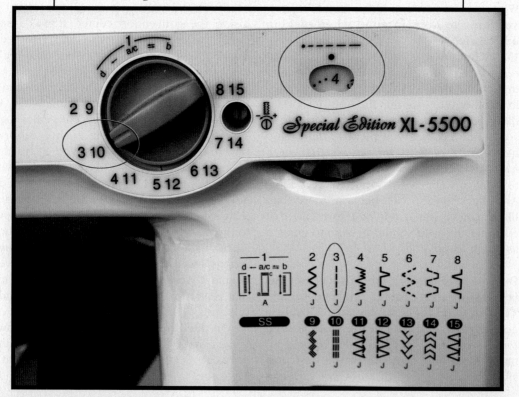

Step 2: Set your tension dial to 0.

Step 3: Sew a vertical line down your fabric. Cut the threads. Then set your tension level to 2. Then sew another vertical line. Cut the threads. Set your tension level to 4… you get the idea. Do this in tension unit increments of 2 till you get to maximum tension. In some instances you may not get to max tension without the thread snapping repeatedly and your machine making sad noises. That's okay, just stop there.

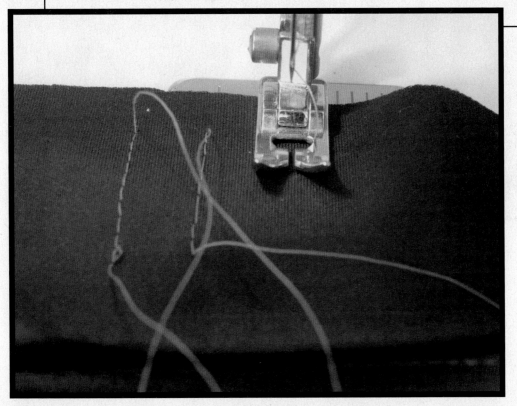

Step 4: Mark your lines with each tension number you used – 0, 2, 4, 5 (my machine's default tension), 6, 8 and 9 in my case. On the top side of the fabric, your stitches might not look too bad...

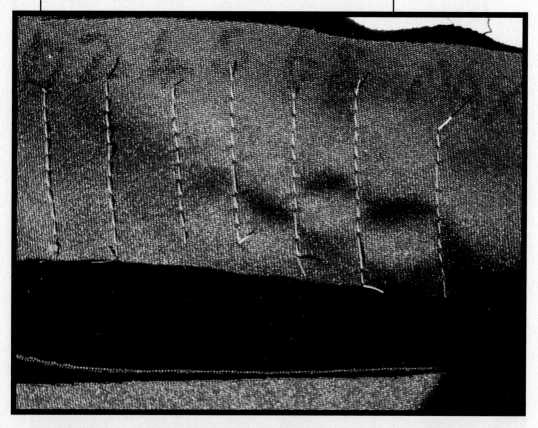

I've really upped the contrast on this picture to bring out the shadows beneath the stitches on tension levels 0 and 2. The thread is sitting loose against the fabric. You don't want that, so those tension levels are no good. See the oval shadows from tension levels 5 and up? That's puckering, caused by the tension being too tight. You don't want those ones either.

Step 5:. Flip your fabric over. Oh dear.

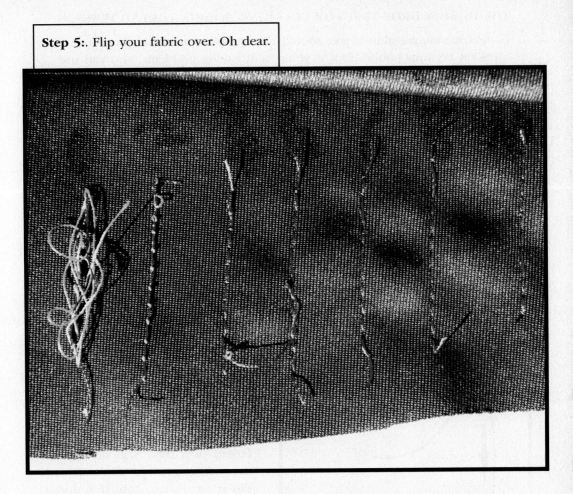

The light blue is the top thread. The more top thread you have showing, the looser the tension is. If you have something like tension level 0 or 1 happening, you will get a birds nest in your feed dogs, snapped thread or even a snapped needle. This is because the tension is so loose that the top thread isn't being pulled back up through the fabric properly and is looping underneath. Seams will just separate when it's like that. Ideally, you want there to be no blue or a tiny dot of blue. This essentially means that the interlock between the top and bottom thread actually sits within the weave of the fabric.

So, which tension to use for this fabric? Well, at tension level 4, there's still some blue dots showing, but at tension level 5, you start to get some puckering, which means the tension is too tight. So for this fabric I'd set the tension dial between 4 and 5.

Every time you work with a new fabric, it's worth doing this. Keep a notebook and write down which fabric types require which tension. Lighter fabrics like silk and chiffon will need a lower tension than heavier fabrics like cotton drill. If you're sewing multiple fabric layers you may also need to adjust the tension accordingly too. If ever in doubt, do a sample like the one above. It takes a few minutes and may save a lot of frustration and cursing at your machine!

THE BOBBIN DROP TEST FOR CHECKING BOBBIN THREAD TENSION

As mentioned above, you should almost never need to adjust thread tension on your bobbin. But if you're still having problems, you can use the bobbin drop test if your machine has a removable bobbin case that you load the bobbin into (most modern machines do), to check bobbin thread tension.

To perform the bobbin drop test, simply load a bobbin into the bobbin case as you would do if you were about to thread up your machine. But instead of putting the bobbin case into the machine, grab hold of the emerging bobbin thread a little above where it comes out of the casing. Hold it up so it dangles. It should not start unspooling. Now, move your hand up, and then move it down forcefully, as if you were dropping a yo-yo.

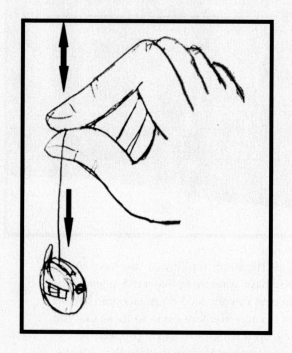

If your bobbin tension is correct, the bobbin will unspool for a short length (less than 5cm or 2 inches depending on how forcefully you did it), and then stop. If it doesn't stop, or you end up with a rather long length of thread between your thumb and the bobbin, then you may need to tighten the tension screw on the bobbin casing a little. The screw is really quite large, as shown in the picture, you won't miss it. Use a small flat-head screwdriver to turn it, you only need to turn it by a mm or so to make a big difference so turn carefully. Repeat the bobbin drop test to make sure you're happy – as I say, it should unspool a short length and then stop. If it doesn't unspool at all, then the tension is too tight and you need to loosen it a little.

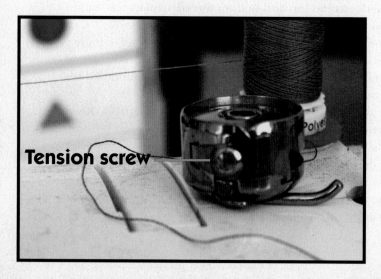

Tension screw

TUTORIAL

ZIPPER INSERTION

by Marianne Coleman (http://www.facebook.com/mazcostuts)

When making costumes, an important consideration is how one gets into and out of said costume. Zips are a really common method, and this tutorial demonstrates a quick and easy method of neatly inserting a zip along a seam. This works for invisible and visible close-ended zips and the zipper teeth are neatly hidden from view.

Step 1: Measure your zip from the very top, to the bottom of the silver end marker, where the zipper will end up when the zip is fully opened.

Step 2: Pin your seam and measure from the top of the seam down as far as the measurement you made in Step 1. Mark with chalk just below this measurement. You will be backstitching here to secure your seam.

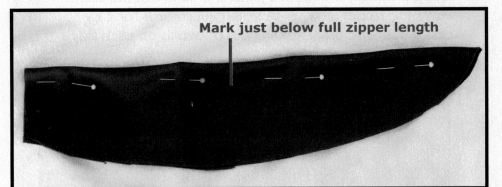

Mark just below full zipper length

Step 3: Set your sewing machine to do a straight stitch and the stitch length to maximum.

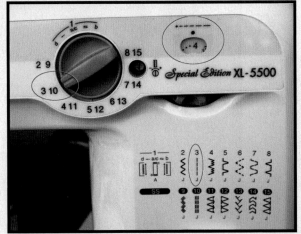

Step 4: Without backstitching the beginning, sew from the top of the seam to your chalk mark. Backstitch at the chalk mark. You will be removing the preceding stitches later on. Then continue your seam right down to the end, backstitching at the end.

Step 5: Lay your fabric out flat with your raw seam edges facing up. Press these flat with an iron.

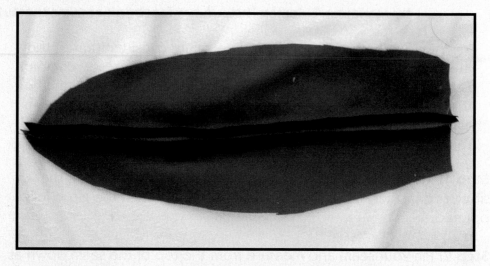

Step 6: With the raw seam side still facing up, lay your zip face down with the teeth against the centre of the seam. Move the zipper lifter so it's pointing upwards for easy access. Put a temporary holding pin or two in on each side.

Step 7: Fit a zipper foot to your sewing machine. Put the bottom end of the zip under the sewing machine and stitch back and forth on it several times to secure the bottom end of the zip centrally over the seam. You should be pretty much stitching on top of where you back-stitched the seam earlier. Doing this creates an easy visual mark for the bottom of the zip for when you go to sew the sides, and secures the bottom part against wear and tear.

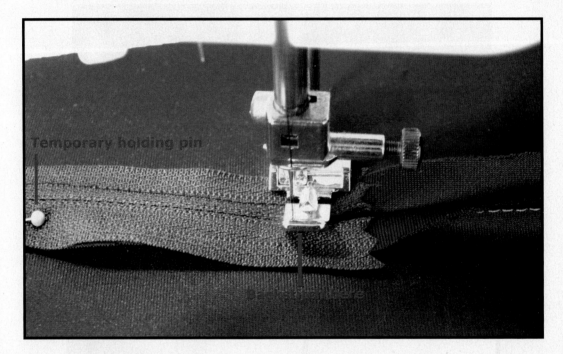

Step 8: Flip the whole thing over and pin the rest of the zip securely into place. You will now be sewing on the top side. Remove the temporary holding pins from beneath. The zipper teeth must remain central on the line of the seam. Move the zipper by pushing down on the zipper lifter until the zip is halfway open.

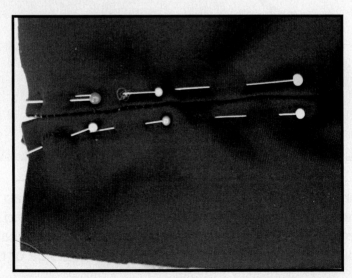

Step 9: Start at the top of the zipper, backstitch and sew until your zipper foot touches the bulk of the zipper – use the central seam line as your guide to stay straight. At this point, with your needle down in the fabric, lift the presser foot up and rotate the fabric sideways until you can grab the zipper lifter. Pull the zipper lifter to close the zip fully, then return the fabric to its original position. This ensures you never have to actually sew past the zipper which creates a bulge in your otherwise straight stitching.

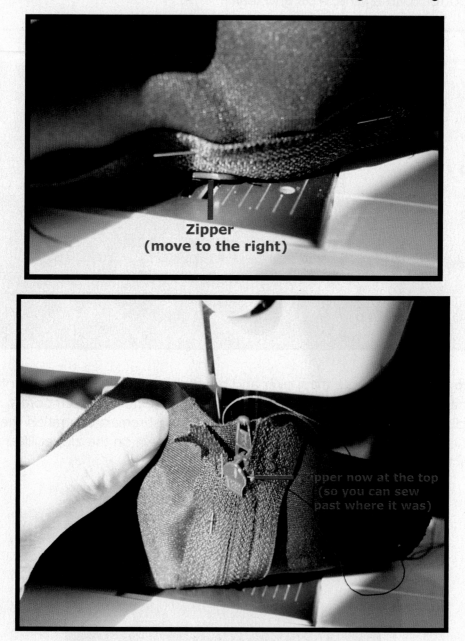

Zipper
(move to the right)

ipper now at the top
(so you can sew
past where it was)

Step 10: Continue sewing down to where you stitched in Step 7, and stop with the needle still in the fabric. Lift the presser foot and turn the fabric 90 degrees, then put the presser foot down again so that you can sew over your stitching from Step 7 to reach the other side of the zip.

Once you get to the end of that little bit of stitching, repeat the same rotation to now start sewing up the other side of the zip. You will need to repeat the zipper movement method described in Step 8 to avoid sewing around the zipper. Backstitch once you have reached the top of the zipper, then cut your threads.

Step 11: Position your seam ripper within the central seam, just above the backstitching that you did in Step 7. Use the seam ripper to rip right the way up the central seam to the top of the zip. You may need to use tweezers to pick out any stray threads to avoid them getting caught in the zipper.

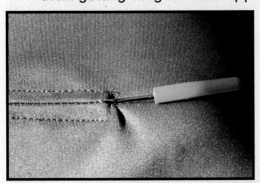
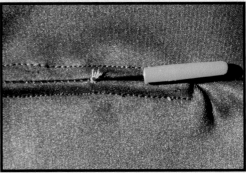

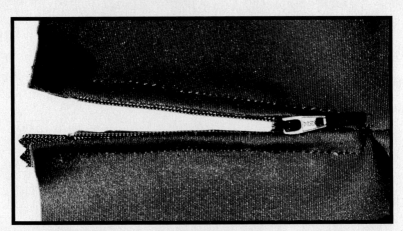

And done! Now you can just hem the top, attach a waistband, whatever you wish to do.

What draws people to cosplay?

Eddie Newsome (EN): I think for every person what draws them to cosplay is different. For some it's the chance to dress as their favorite characters or group, while others do it as an expression of identification or to pay homage to an artist or writer, while others do it as a badge of pride or honor of a character that embodies a historical or fictional aspect that they are proud of, the list goes on and on.

Can you describe your first experience with cosplay?

EN: My first experience with cosplay was at San Diego Comic Con. It was great to be at the mecca of geekdom, to see all the people in costume while I was in mine and feeling like it was just the daily norm.

What was your first costume?

EN: My first costume was Isaiah Bradley, the first black Captain America. I read that book, *Truth: Red, White, and Black,* by Kyle Baker and Robert Morales and was instantly drawn to the story and the character. Isaiah Bradley has become my favorite costume over the years as well.

What's the best experience you have had as a cosplayer?

EN: I have many, but one was when I met Kyle Baker at San Diego Comic Con dressed as Isaiah Bradley. It's a cosplayer's dream to meet the creator, artist or writer of the character they are dressed as and get the thumbs up, and he was very happy to see it.

Another was when I dressed as Future Static Shock, created by Dwayne McDuffie. I had had spoken online with him and told him that I was working on the costume and that he was my inspiration. Sadly, he passed the year that I was finally ready to debut it. But to get the thumbs up from the Milestone crew as well the voice of young Static, Phillip Lamarr, as well as his creator, Michael Davis, was good. And to finally meet Dwayne's widow a few years later in the costume and to see her get emotional over the costume and tell me how he would have been proud – it made it all worthwhile that I paid homage to the man and the vision.

Cosplay seems to be enjoying a new level in popularity. Can you isolate a certain event or events that caused the increase in popularity?

EN: I can't really isolate a specific time, but I can say the popularity of TV shows, movies and resurgence of comics has helped the cause. Geek culture as a whole being more embraced these days has done a lot as well.

Do you see any specific cosplay trends right now?

EN: That's the beauty of cosplay. It's not about trends, but more about expression and appreciation.

What do you see in the future for cosplay?

EN: The future of cosplay is what we want it to be. Anytime you can walk onto a convention floor and see costumes that look better than the version you see on the big screen – that should tell you something. I was an introvert who didn't go to my high school prom, and the term "geek" and "nerd" were badges of shame. Fast-forward to now and I'm not only a co-author of a cosplay book but I've met great people along the way! So what do I see for the future of cosplay? Growth, evolution, and acceptance.

MASKS & HELMETS

By Britany Marriott

A lot of people use different techniques when it comes to building armor. This one came into fruition when I was looking for things around my house I can utilize instead of over-stretching my budget with fancier materials.

Lightweight cardboard can be a sturdy, inexpensive, easy, and versatile base for any armor, especially for fantasy armor that have exaggerated shapes and outlandish curves you won't see in life. With this technique, the armor is much lighter and easier to move in, especially during a convention where normal functions can become bothersome if armor is in the way. Even though this tutorial is based off of one item, the technique can be used for so many other pieces, from shields to shoe covers.

Here are the items you'll need:
- Cardboard
- Masking Tape and Packaging Tape
- Hot glue
- Newspaper
- Mod Podge
- Paper
- Pencil or Pen
- Acrylic paint and acrylic gesso
- Epoxy resin
- Measuring tape
- Dremmel or sandpaper

Step 1: Measure the diameter of your head with your measuring tape (from your forehead to where your spine and skull connect. Then measure the circumference of your head as well. If you plan on wearing a wig with it, add an extra half-inch to 1-inch to your measurements depending on the thickness of your wig, or just measure with the wig on if you have the wig on-hand.

Step 2: Prep your workspace so it is easier to work on. Take some of your cardboard and cover it with packaging tape. This will help with your project not sticking to your workplace and having paint peel off or cardboard sticking and drying to your finished product.

Step 3: Cut your cardboard into long strips. My cardboard was about 8 inches wide by 12 inches long, so I cut them to about a half-inch wide and 12 inches long, giving me about 16 stripe per piece.

Step 4: Connect a couple of strips together lengthwise to match your head's circumference. Once you're done with that, connect a long piece of cardboard from the front of your helmet to the back to get your diameter. Make sure it fits a bit loosely; you're going to be building off of what you're starting with.

Step 5: Begin taking your long strips and crisscross them until you have most of the surface area covered. This will give you an even base to build off of. There will be some holes, but that is perfectly fine.

Step 6: For this mask, I needed to make cat ears, so I made cones out of paper. You can use this technique for other sorts of protruding details. I also used newspaper to stuff the ears to give them more stability. Place any of these sort of details on the helmet and glue them down.

Step 7: Begin wrapping the entire helmet in masking tape. This step is all about building stability for your build. Make sure there is no cardboard left uncovered in your helmet. I wouldn't use duct tape or anything too slippery for this part of your helmet because you'll be building off of it; you want your materials to stick.

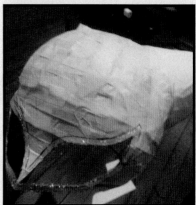

Step 8: Once you have the base of your helmet, take a piece of paper and create a stencil for the eye holes (if your project requires them). Temporarily tape them on and build the eye holes with left over pieces of cardboard. Take the eye template off once you've gotten your eye holes, and cover them in masking tape.

Step 9: If you're adding any other details that should protrude a bit, add those to your helmet with hot glue and extra cardboard. As you can see, it bellows out in the photo to give it more dimension – you can use extra hot glue here to make it stand out even more.

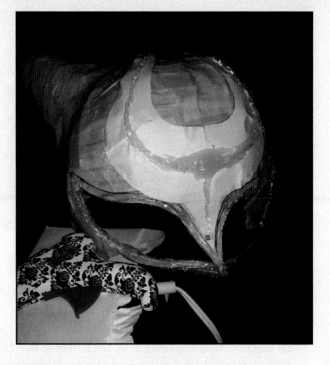

Step 10: Once you're done wrap the entire helmet with newspaper that's wet with mod podge. Make sure you pay attention to the creases in your helmet; the newspaper must not bellow out unnaturally and must be properly tucked around corners and edges of your work.

Step 11: Once the mod podge is dried, use a dremmel to shave down bumpy parts to get a nice even finish. Sand paper is also fine, but it's going to take a while to get the bumps out compared to the dremmel.

Step 12: Paint your helmet. I used acrylic paint and a gesso. Gesso is a waterproof base which I used because I will be sweating a lot using this helmet in the late summer with a wig on; it's good to use Gesso as a base anyway to give your paint a more even look compared to painting directly on the newspaper. Acrylic paint will also be great for this project because it gives a nice shine when it dries.

Step 13: At this point the helmet is extremely sturdy and if you would like to apply a thin layer of resin inside the helmet as well as outside, it will give it a polished look similar to an actual helmet.

TUTORIAL

WORBLA 101

By
Katie
Fleming

Regular Worbla, AKA Worbla's Finest Art, is magical stuff. With a little time and patience, one can create impressive, realistic, and lightweight cosplay armor and accessories. Worbla is a thermoplastic sold in sheets that when heated to a certain temperature – usually around 90 degrees Celsius or 194 degrees Fahrenheit – will become moldable. It is a costly material, but it can create beautiful, show stopping pieces!

Patterning: Before you begin using Worbla, you'll need to get your basic shapes and patterns ready that correspond to your character or item design. Below is a very basic tutorial on patterning to give you an idea on how to get started. You may wish to research more advanced pattern making resources.

For patterning you'll need:

- **Plastic Wrap**
- **Duct, Masking, or Painters tape**
- **Scissors**
- **Marker**
- **An Assistant**

Step 1: Wrap area of body with plastic wrap that you wish to have armor. This is simply so that the tape does not stick to your skin.

Step 2: Cover the plastic wrap area with the tape of your choice. This is where an assistant may come in handy, especially for parts of the body that are hard to reach.

Step 3: Draw a line down the center of where the underside of the piece will be. You or your assistant should very carefully and slowly cut down the line.

Step 4: Remove the piece. Ta-da! You now have a basic pattern! You can now draw directly on the pattern the shape that corresponds to your character.

Step 5: Cut out this pattern to transfer onto your foam.

Materials and Tools:

- Worbla
- Heat gun
- Sharp scissors
- Aluminum foil and/or a heat resistant surface
- A marker (Sharpies are fantastic!)
- Foam: This solely depends on the desired thickness of your armor – I recommend craft foam or EVA foam.

Prepare your surface: Heat guns reach extremely high temperatures that can easily burn or melt surfaces like carpet, wood, or plastics. Steer clear of having flammable items nearby. Worbla will also stick to other plastics. The simplistic way to avoid this is to lay a couple layers of aluminum foil down on the surface you are working on and set aside other materials away from work area.

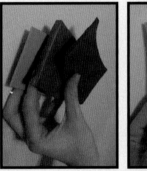

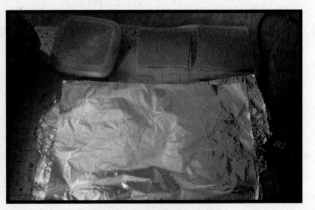

Step 1: Transfer your pattern onto the foam and cut out with scissors.

Step 2: Cut a piece of Worbla slightly larger than your foam piece (about 1/4-1/2 inch extra on all sides).

Step 3: Lay the Worbla down on your prepared surface.

Step 4: Hold heat gun approximately five inches away from Worbla piece, turn on, and move back and forth evenly over the Worbla surface. The Worbla will darken slightly, develop a wet look surface and become limp.

Use caution when touching the Worbla after heating. Be mindful as to not heat the Worbla too much. It can burn, become too hot to touch, and/or cause bubbling. If this happens, wait a few minutes to cool. You can flatten bubbles by puncturing them with a needle and pressing on the area gently to smooth it out.

Step 5: Once Worbla is heated to a proper temperature, lay your foam piece on top, making sure it's centered.

Step 6: Working quickly before the Worbla cools completely, fold the edges of the Worbla over the foam. You can reheat if needed, but distribute heat evenly or else your foam will burn.

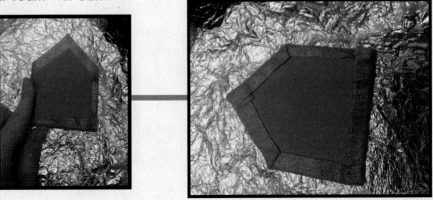

Step 7: While Worbla is still warm, carefully pick up the piece, and shape it to fit over the body area. Reheat as needed. Avoid heating directly over the foam.

Step 8: Now that you have your basic shape, you can add details!

Detailing your Worbla: In a nutshell, Worbla sticks to Worbla. It is an adhesive to itself. No glue required! You can cut strips and shapes out of worbla, heat them slightly and stick them directly to your armor to create awesome three-dimensional effects. Use your imagination or follow the design of your beloved character! There is no limit as to what you can create. Below are some examples of details added before painting. Feel free to draw directly on the Worbla to get an idea of what you want!

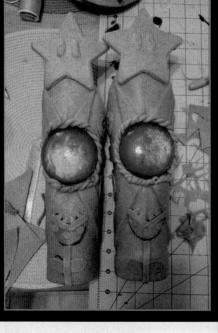

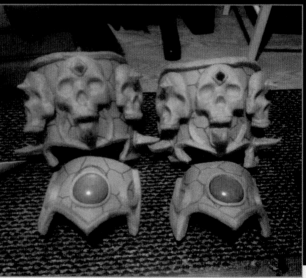

Priming and Painting Worbla: Worbla on its own has a very rough, bumpy texture. Unless you want that rough look, you'll need to prep your pieces prior to paint. To get a smoother look, there are many ways to prep your armor pieces. The most common and perhaps most accessible and simplistic is to prime your Worbla with wood glue. Give your Worbla pieces several coats, about four to six layers of wood glue, letting each layer dry before applying another. This will leave your armor with a smoother, armor-like surface. Sanding, gesso, shellac, and resin are various other methods to prep your Worbla pieces.

The Worbla Scraps: One of the best things about Worbla is that you never waste it. Always keep your scrap pieces! You can use them for the small details or you can heat a pile of them up and mold them into a lot of cool things! For Example: Worbla scraps were used to make the tips of the arrows below!

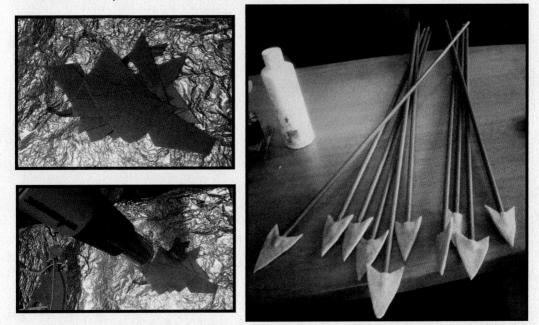

Where to buy this stuff: Worbla itself can be found from a number of online retailers. Craft foam can be found at most craft and hobby stores, while thicker EVA foam can be found at hardware and home improvement stores. Heat guns can also be found at most hardware stores.

To conclude: Now you have some basic knowledge of Worbla! You are on your way to creating some amazing Worbla armor and accessories! It is all about trial and error, so give it a shot and do not hesitate to experiment and tap into your imagination. Remember that this community is full of talented and knowledgeable cosplayers that are willing to share what they know. We are here for you!

Cosplayer Spotlight: Fan Service Thor

Please introduce yourself!

Eric Kays (EK): My name is Eric Kays, but my cosplay persona is "Fan Service Thor." I'm a freelance social media and transmedia developer and I recently graduated with a degree in film and television. I currently live in Atlanta, Georgia.

What is your approach to cosplay? How do you go about putting together the costumes?

EK: As a new person to costume creation, I'm literally making up my process as I go along. Sometimes I take something someone else has done - there's a great tutorial on Tumblr I used to create my muscle suit for my Thor costume - and sometimes I look at the options and say "screw it, I'm using hot glue and seeing where this goes!" I plan on taking courses and continuing to educate myself to figure out how to be less wasteful of materials and more intentional with design.

What is one of the best and most memorable experiences you've had with cosplay?

EK: There are a number of experiences that have been incredible: my experience at Dragon Con was the first time I had trouble moving from one location to another from the amount of attention I gained, or the several times I've arm wrestled Gaston at Disney World. My most memorable experience, however, comes from Disney World when I was still walking around in a t-shirt and a cape made of duck cloth from Wal-Mart. People were continually calling out "Thor!" as I would walk by, so I got used to hearing the name and responding to it. Around 11 PM that night, I once again heard it, and turned around. A mother with a boy about four or five years-old ran up to me and told me that her son had been denied the opportunity to ride Space Mountain because of his height. She then went on to explain that he had seen me and wanted to get a picture with Thor.

This was one of the key moments for me that solidified one of the reasons I love cosplay and especially love dressing as Thor so much. There's always going to be people who want to take pictures of me or want to get pictures with me, but the opportunity to get a picture with a child who sees you as the character you represent, instead of just another great cosplayer, is far more special to me.

What was one of your worst?

EK: I think I've been really fortunate in my short time cosplaying because I don't really have a "horrible" experience to talk about. I have, however, noticed a trend with people breaking unspoken boundaries with me in cosplay. I adhere to the rule that you do not touch another cosplayer or their props without their permission.

In my experience, however, almost every convention I've been to, someone, in most cases a woman, has approached me and started touching my hair without asking me. Believe me, I get it. My hair is glorious and needs to be touched. But my hair is a part of my body and I don't want people to touch it without permission. Man or woman, cosplay is not consent. I will note, though, that if you ask and aren't terribly creepy about it, I'm probably not going to say no. I am Fan Service Thor, after all!

TUTORIAL

Circle Skirts

By Carrie Wood

Circle skirts are not only a great beginner sewing project, but is also extremely versatile. It's also great for many different cosplays! Circle skirts can be made out of plenty of different materials, in nearly any length necessary, and are applicable for plenty of different situations. It's incredible how once you nail down how to make fabric circles, doors really open up for you in a lot of different and creative ways!

Materials:

- Measuring tape
- Fabric scissors
- Calculator
- Chalk pencil or fabric marker
- Fabric of your choice (length depending entirely on how long you need the skirt to be – we generally recommend thicker fabrics so that you don't have to make a lining for it, too)

Step 1: Figure out where you want the hem of the skirt to land. Though there's plenty of room for creativity here in terms of hems – uneven hems, patterned hems and so on – for the sake of this tutorial we're going with a basic straight hem. Once you decide the length of your choice, bust out your measuring tape and measure from your waist to that length (it might help to have help here). Note this down as your length measurement.

Step 2: You need to figure out your waist radius. This is not your waist in inches (that's actually your waist circumference). A little bit of math is needed here – that's what the calculator is for! Measure around your waist (or hips), wherever the skirt will need to sit once it's completed. Divide this number by pi (3.14), and divide that final number by 2. This is your waist radius – note that number down as well.

Step 3: Lay your fabric out flat and determine the center point along the fold. Use your fabric marker or chalk (we're using a pen so you can see our marks here) to mark this point.

Step 4: Using your measuring tape, swing a half-circle around the halfway point in the fabric at the measurement you reached for your waist radius. Or, as we're doing here, use a piece of embroidery floss measured to the appropriate length and swing that around. We find that the string sometimes cooperates better than a stiff measuring tape!

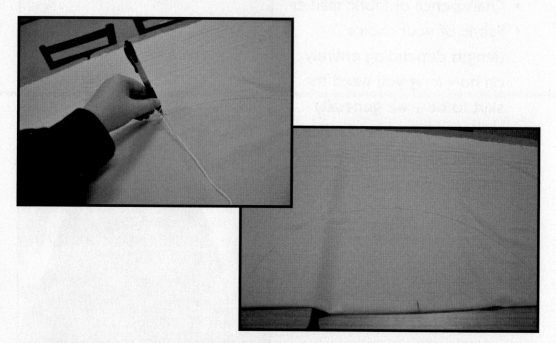

Step 5: Next, still with either measuring tape or floss at the right length, swing another circle around at the skirt length measurement – so you'll need to add the skirt length measurement to the waist radius measurement to get the correct length. You should now have a piece of fabric with two half-circles on it.

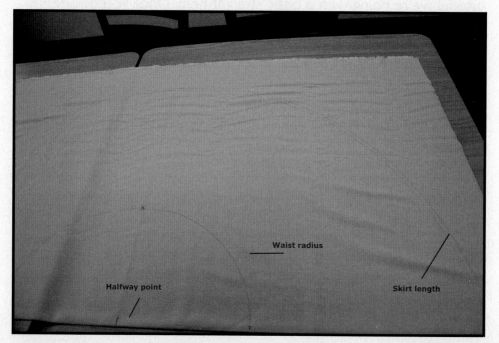

Step 6: Cut out your pattern and un-fold it. You should have one large circular piece of fabric. Congratulations, you've done most of the work already!

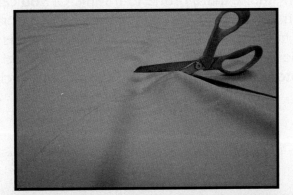

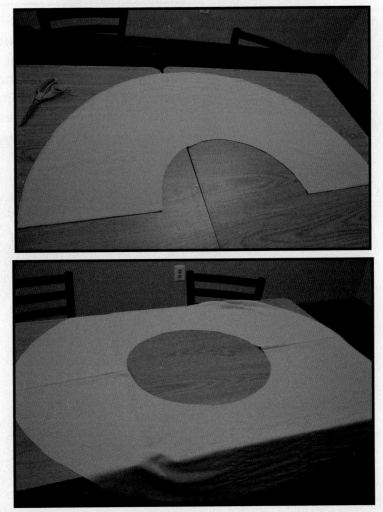

Step 7: From here, you probably will want to make a waistband and insert a closure of some sort, whether that is a zipper (for zipper insertion, please see the tutorial elsewhere in this very book!), elastic, or snaps. If you're using a stretchy material like spandex, you might not even need to do anything beyond making a waistband.

Step 8: You probably want to hem the bottom of your skirt, assuming you're using fabric that's prone to fraying. Or you can add a nice trim, or do whatever you'd like! You're pretty much done at this point unless you're trying to get fancy with it by adding layers or by making the waist wider and then gathering it for a more ruffled effect – we've included photos of both gathered and ungathered circle skirts here.

Having a good circle skirt in your repertoire can come in handy for a number of projects, as you can see from the examples of finished ones that I – and many of my friends – have made over the years!

Gathered skirt

Ungathered skirt

THE LOGO

By Mark Huesman

The Flash #239 (Feb. 1976)
©DC Comics

The logo, the sigil, the insignia, the crest... that eye-catching graphic design element is usually found in the center of the hero's chest. It can be one of the final steps in making a costume, and you don't have to be Paul Gambi (this book needed at least one mention of Central City's tailor extraordinaire) to make it look good.

Materials: Computer with printer and basic image editing software, (if not a computer, then graph paper), scissors, tacky spray, markers, sewing machine, steam iron, and the lettering material (felt, athletic twill, any stiff fabric).

Marvel Studios photo

Step 1 - Getting the pattern: Thanks to the internet, what was once a separate artistic challenge is now all too easy. Typing in a search for "logo (character name)" should provide you with the design ready to re-size to your needs for your costume. Your basic image-editing software should be used to flip the design to appear as a mirror image. Then you can print it out and hold it up to your costume to establish which size looks best in the mirror. You can quickly tweak the size by 5-10% larger or smaller to find that perfect size and avoid conflicts with seams and/or zippers. Once that is settled, print 1 copy of the mirror image plus one copy for each color of the design. The SHIELD logo with white graphics on a black background will be used for the demonstration, so 2 mirror printouts will be needed. Doing a classic Superman logo would require 3 (red plus yellow plus 1).

Step 2: Flip the design back to un-mirrored and print one copy of that as a reference.

The logo patch material: While felt is a common fabric for logos, athletic twill is more durable and gives a shine. Professional sports teams use it for numbering (and it was used for this tutorial) and it has the benefit of a heat-activated adhesive backing. The grooves catch the light differently at different angles, so keep the orientation of the grooves consistent.

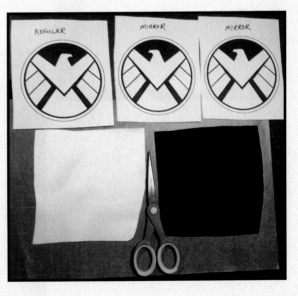

Step 3: Number the pieces on all the print-outs. If the numbers go counter-clockwise on the mirror patterns, be sure to go clockwise on the regular reference print-out. Underline the number so you know which way is down. On the outer ring, mark the top of the circle.

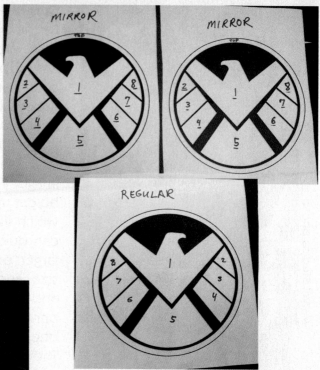

Step 4: Using a tacky spray, apply a 2-3 second burst onto the back of one of the mirror patterns. Put some newspaper behind the mirror paper and have some ventilation in the room.

Step 5: Place the sticky sprayed side of the mirror pattern paper against the back side of the patch material.

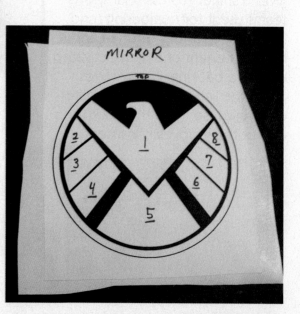

Step 6: Cut the individual pieces (it's better to cut slightly inside the line [making the pieces a wee bit smaller] to compensate for the thread on the edge).

Don't peel away the paper backing just yet. Match the cut pieces to the numbers on the intact mirror printout to keep it organized.

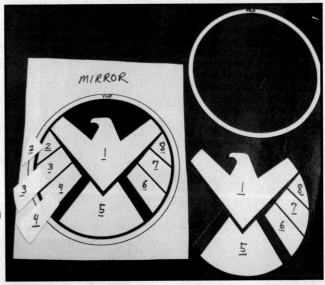

With everything cut, you can now check to verify that all the pieces are present.

Step 7: Peel the paper and place the various pieces in the proper location. If you have a light table, you can place the background fabric over the regular print-out... and that's not cheating.

If you're using felt, peel up an edge of each piece and squirt some glue underneath to stick it in place. For athletic twill, put a piece of paper over the design and use an iron on a medium setting. No steam is needed.

Step 8: Time to sew. You'll want to use a zig-zag stitch, with a width of 2 millimeters, and a stitch frequency of 24 stitches per inch. Basic all-purpose thread is fine. No need to use the shiny embroidery thread.

Most of the choices for patch fabric are pretty forgiving, so if you accidently steer off course, you can remove the wayward stitching and sew along the edge again.

Now it's all sewn except for the outer white ring. Excess threads have been cut away. The patch is ready for trimming.

Step 9: A quick scissor trim around the edge gives you the final patch ready to be added to your costume.

The same process can be used to add lettering around a design, so your logo could be a nice display piece to be framed instead of worn.

Or you could have something unique to be autographed by your favorite comic creator.

Cosplayer Spotlight: Katie Fleming

What was it about cosplay that made you want to participate?

Katie Fleming (KF): The cosplay world was introduced to me after I started volunteer acting at a local haunted house about eight years ago. I tagged along with them to some horror conventions and would wear their original costumes to help advertise the haunt. But it wasn't until after I attended New York Comic Con in 2012 that I actually tried cosplaying myself! The creative atmosphere and the idea of becoming a new character for the day is seriously amazing, and is what truly got me hooked on cosplay! It allows you to become a new personality and step away from the norms a bit. It can be a huge stress reliever and extremely fun!

What is your approach to cosplay? How do you go about putting together your costumes?

KF: Cosplay just sort of happens for me. If I see a character that truly catches my attention, I latch onto it like a leech and never let go! It may be one that I have admired all my life, or one recently introduced to me. You'll have to yank hard to get my mind off of it. I then meditate and mentally prepare myself for the pressure and empty wallet that will lie ahead (laughs). No, but in all seriousness, I do plan and budget everything first. I question how difficult it is going to be, what materials I'll need, how much money it'll cost me, and so on. If it is within my means, I'll tackle the project! If it isn't, it just goes on my list of dream cosplays. A cosplay idea never truly leaves my head.

What is one of the best and most memorable experiences you've had with cosplay?
KF: I could go on and on about the positive aspects of cosplay. There are so many awesome moments! But I'd have to say that seeing the kids' reactions to your cosplay is the best. They truly believe you are this character standing there in real life that they have only seen in video games, movies, or television. I have had multiple children ask my character for their autograph and you can just see their eyes light up! I try my best to stay in character which makes for even a greater interaction with them! Those are the moments I cherish the most.

What do you think cosplay adds to the overall convention experience?
KF: Cosplay makes the convention experience even more exciting! For non-cosplayers and cosplayers, what is better than seeing your beloved characters in real life? It is a form of entertainment that brings unity to fandoms of all types. You can immediately recognize a person that enjoys exactly what you enjoy and that can result in new relationships and interactions that may not have happened without it! There is such a feeling of acceptance and appreciation in the world of cosplay because outside of the convention world, this culture isn't always appreciated, so we must embrace it!

CONTOURING –
USING LIGHT AND SHADOW TO
CHANGE THE SHAPE OF YOUR FACE

This tutorial will introduce you to the basics of contouring, a makeup technique that uses light and shadow to trick the eye (and camera) into believing that the shape of your face has changed. This is especially useful for female-to-male cross-play and characters with angular and older faces. However, contouring should be in your arsenal for nearly every character you cosplay. Cameras and masquerade stage lights will "flatten" the appearance of your face, and it's a good idea to artificially accentuate the highlights and shadows of your own face even if you aren't changing the shape of any of your facial features.

You will need:
- Foundation in your base color.

- Matte eyeshadow, creme foundation, or concealer 2 shades darker than your base skin color ("shadow") Don't go too dark with your shadow color! Using a shadow color that is too dark will lead to the dreaded "dirt face" look that is often seen in female-to-male cross-play.

- Matte eyeshadow, creme foundation, or concealer two shades lighter than your base skin color ("highlight"). If you are pale like I am, this color will likely be white. If your character is particularly feminine and/or youthful, you may use a highlight with a slight shimmer or sparkle.

- Note: Contouring palettes do exist, but if your skin is especially light or especially dark, the colors included in the palette likely won't work for you. Test them in the store before you buy them.

- Note the Second: If you are painting your skin a different color, you will ALWAYS need to contour to counteract the "flattening" effect of face paint. Find colors 1-2 shades darker and lighter than your base body paint and follow the directions as below.

- A makeup sponge to blend your contours. They make sponges with rounded edges especially for blending, but you can use a triangular makeup sponge as long as you avoid the edges/corners.

- Translucent setting powder.

The rest of the makeup you use (e.g. blush, eyeliner, eyeshadow, mascara) depends on what gender and type of character you will be cosplaying.

Part One: General Concepts

The goal of contouring is to artificially add highlights and shadows to trick the viewer's eye into believing that the actual architecture of your face has changed. To do this, you need a brief understanding of how light hits the face. Here is a photo of my face with little to no makeup (eek!) and the flash on to accentuate the highlights (yellow) and shadows (blue) on my face.

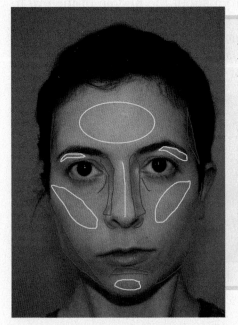

As you can see, parts of the face that stick out – the nose, forehead, cheekbones, and chin – are highlighted because the light hits them directly. As a result, these facial features also cast a shadow on the rest of the face. Shadows are sharper around more angular parts of the face and softer around more rounded parts of the face – therefore, adding sharper/linear shapes will make the face appear more angular, whereas softer/curved contouring shapes will soften your facial features. For contouring, we will pretend that the "lighting" is perfectly centered on our face and slightly above our head, as is true of most ambient light.

Part Two: Defining Each Facial Feature

Now that you have an idea of how light hits each part of the face, you can now create highlights and shadows to alter the shape of certain facial features. For this section, I'll go through an example of how I do my contouring for Professor Sycamore from Pokémon X/Y.

While this particular example is for female-to-male crossplay, I'll explain how to use contouring to make a wide variety of changes to your facial structure. It's easiest to think about each facial feature separately.

Start by applying your foundation and, if applicable, setting it with powder. You will want moderate to full coverage to make your face as blank a slate as possible. All other makeup should wait until you are finished contouring.

General Face Shape: What shape is your character's face? Is it long or short? Is it oval, square, round, or heart-shaped? Is it narrower at the top, bottom, or neither? How prominent is their jaw? What shape is it?

Professor Sycamore has a long, somewhat narrow face with a very square jawbone (mandible). I will make a soft shadow symmetrically on both sides of the face to narrow my face and a sharp shadow around my jawbone and under my chin, which are slightly rounded. This shadow makes them look both more prominent and more square.

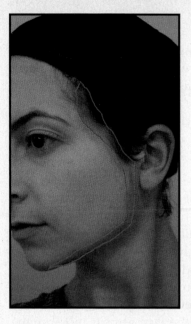

Brow/Forehead: This is not necessary for most female characters, but many masculine characters have a strong, prominent brow. This brow bone is technically formed by the upper edge of the eye sockets and is just below the eyebrows. In order to fake a prominent brow, add shadows on either side of the uppermost part of the nose as well as along the brow bone from about the middle of the eye to the outer edge of the eye. Even if you do not do this step, add a symmetrical highlight along the entirety of your forehead and two highlights along the most prominent part of your brow bones.

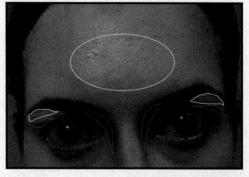

Nose: Look at the shape of your character's nose. Is it narrow? Wide? Is there a prominent bump in the middle or bulb at the tip of the nose? Does it look like a rectangle, triangle, or inverted triangle? If you are contouring your brow bone, continue the contour lines you started along either side of your nose. If not, start contouring lines slightly below where you would begin to contour the brow bone. These contouring lines will always be straight (save the bump or bulb as mentioned before), but they can be at an angle if the character's nose is narrower or wider at the bottom. Lightly shade in the sides with your shadow color, then add a highlight down the center of your nose.

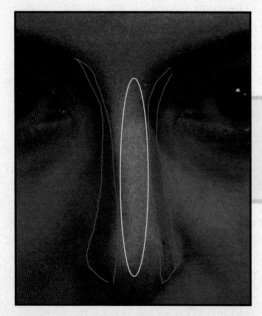

Sycamore has a fairly petite nose, and my own nose is slightly beaky, so I drew contour lines at the natural sides of my nose and just over the edges of the tip of my nose to minimize it.

Eyes: Does the character have a single or double eyelid? How hooded or deep-set are their eyes? If the character's eyes are deep-set, use your shadow color along the crease of your eyelid if you have a double eyelid, or where the crease would be if you have a single eyelid. I'll go over under-eye bags/wrinkles below. Add a highlight on the eyelid itself.

Like Sycamore, I also have fairly hooded eyes and a double eyelid, so there's not too much I need to do in this respect.

Cheekbones: The cheekbones (or zygomatic arches if you're feeling fancy) start slightly below the temples and angle down to the fleshy part of your cheeks approximately at nostril level. Characters with prominent cheekbones will have a strong linear highlight/shadow above and below the cheekbones, whereas characters with fleshy/round cheeks will have a rounded highlight over the "apples" of the cheeks and a more curved shadow. The shadow below the cheekbones that stops 1/2 to 2/3 of the way to the center of the face; this is less present or even absent in characters with very round faces. This is (in my opinion) the hardest shadow to draw realistically, so make sure to practice.

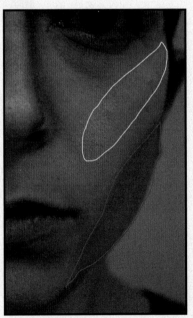

When cosplaying masculine characters with more "chiseled" faces, I like to angle the cheekbone shadow down toward my chin and lightly fill in the sides with the shadow color. Be careful not to make this too dark, or it will just look dirty and unrealistic!

Chin: If your character has a prominent chin, there will be a curved shadow under the lower lip pointing toward the chin, and the tip of the chin will be strongly highlighted. Sycamore's chin is angled at the bottom but is not very prominent, so I'll barely add a shadow there, with a highlight at the point of the chin.

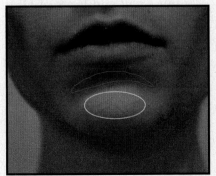

(Optional) Neck/Adam's Apple: More masculine characters will often have an Adam's apple, which is caused by the outline of the larynx bulging out from the neck. You can also add definition to the sternocleidomastoids, which are the two muscles angling down from the neck to the sternum that allow you to turn your head. In order to locate these muscles, turn your head to the side, and the tendons will protrude slightly.

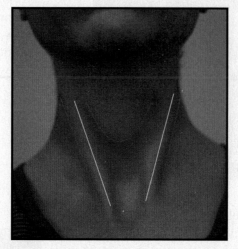

Part Three: Aging

If a character is significantly older than you are, you may want to incorporate aging makeup into your contouring. As we get older, our skin becomes less elastic and begins to wrinkle. There are four main areas where wrinkles form: the forehead, under the eyes, at the outer corner of the eyes ("crow's feet"), and on either side of the nose (nasolabial folds). Even if a character isn't old, if they're constantly tired or sick, they may have under-eye circles or puffy under-eye "bags" that can be detailed very similarly. The main difference between wrinkles and other contouring is that the lines are thinner and sharper. They start narrow at one end, widen slightly in the middle, and taper down on the other end. I use a narrow brush to draw them on.

Sycamore is likely in his mid-to-late thirties, so I won't go crazy, but I will add hints of all these wrinkles:

Part Four: Blending

This is by far the MOST CRUCIAL part of contouring. Blending makes your contouring look natural and believable and corrects for any inconsistencies in your original makeup application (no one's perfect). Take your makeup sponge and gently blend in small circles. Smooth out the sharp edges of the lines you drew earlier. Make sure the entire area of shadow is 1 uniform color. It can also be helpful to dust some pressed powder in the same color as your base foundation over the entire contouring job in order to even out extremes in color.

Here are my completed contours before and after blending:

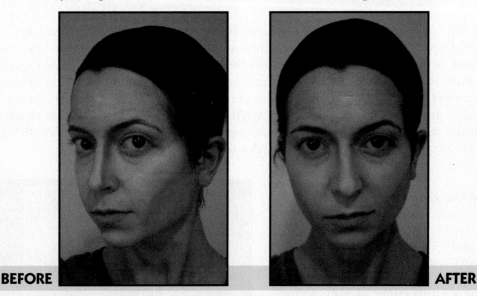

BEFORE   AFTER

Once you've finished your contouring and blending, set everything with translucent setting powder before you move on to eye make-up, blush (if needed), brows, and lip color.

Et voilà! You are now a ruggedly handsome Pokémon professor!

Or, y'know, whatever other character you used this tutorial for. Enjoy your newfound transformative powers!

COSPLAYING SAFELY

By Eddie Newsome

In the cosplay world, safety is absolutely paramount, with invasions of personal space in and around conventions increasing to the point where the "Cosplay is Not Consent" movement needed to begin. Should you have to look over your shoulder constantly while in costume, as if danger is lurking around any corner? No, you shouldn't, and in a perfect world it wouldn't be necessary – but these are the times we live in. So, what can we do, and how can we all have fun while still feeling safe? The following tips are my advice for what a cosplayer should do while at a convention in order to feel worry-free.

1. When out in costume, especially in a non-convention space, live by the law of two at all times. If you have someone with you watching your back, it's less likely that anything will happen to either of you. Some people will take this rule to apply to women only, but that isn't what I'm talking about. This applies to any age, race or gender; I've personally been at conventions where someone was hurt or approached in a not-so-positive way, and when the smoke cleared, they were alone. If you *must* travel alone, be sure that you're aware of where security is.

2. We all have the right to dress as who we desire, but in doing so, it's important to be aware that some will take it in a negative or even in a sexual way. Whether you're a scantily-clad character, or one that has some negative historical ties, there could be some type of backlash – so always be aware of who, where, and what you cosplay.

3. Conventions have taken to posting signs and notices around the show floor to inform that the con is a harassment-free zone, and enforce that "Cosplay is Not Consent." But this idea does not apply only to cosplayers, but to *any attendee* of any gender or race that may feel as though their well-being or their personal space is being intruded upon by a photographer, an interviewer, or fellow attendee. Before attending a convention, find out if they do or do not adhere to a zero-tolerance policy. You should also find out what the procedures are to filing a complaint, and what, according to their guidelines, are actionable offenses.

4. Cosplaying safely doesn't just apply to harassment or feeling uncomfortable; it also applies to your physical safety while in costume, as well as the safety of those around you. If you don't have a clear line of sight, or if your costume is bulky and maneuverability is slow and cumbersome, having someone with you is an absolute must in order to prevent potential injuries to yourself or any patron of the convention.

5. Never be afraid to ask for help! I can't count the times I've been at a convention where a cosplayer has asked for help to either get from point A to point B, or maybe are experiencing a costume malfunction, or are just looking to avoid confrontation. I've been asked to help them fix something, or escort them somewhere, or simply watch their back. The cosplay and convention community is a family in many ways, and chances are there's someone willing to lend a hand if you need it.

6. If you're new to a particular con, try to prepare by asking past attendees how the show is in regards to security in and around the show to get a better feel as to what to expect.

Being safe and having the most enjoyable cosplayer and convention experience is up to all of us. Be sure to have friends or family with you at the con as much as possible – stick to the buddy system and be sure to have a way to get in touch in case of an emergency. Remember, even though you may dress like someone who has superpowers or cool gadgets, *you* don't really have those. Be safe and always watch out for your fellow cosplayers!

Cosplayer Diary: Who Are You?

By Eddie Newsome

Costume – check. Convention tickets – check. Hotel and transportation – check. Now comes the fun part: to be the character you are cosplaying. To me, this is second only to the costume itself in terms of importance in regards to cosplay.

Research is the key in trying to define who you are going to be, and how others will perceive you when in costume. There are so many tools out there to use in crafting your persona, from the television, film or comic book the character might come from, and of course the internet as well. When I decided to cosplay Black Panther from Marvel Comics fame, I was already a fan of the comic book and took the design from the run done by Ken Lashley and Reggie Hudlin. But, a comic book was just one dimension of the character that I had at my disposal. I wanted to see how T'Challa walked, talked, and gestured.

My process when I'm in costume is not simply to emulate the physical attributes, but also to embody their spirit and personality. To make any character believable, this is a must, but it also needs to be open to interpretation. I have seen just as many over-the-top cosplayers in regards to being in-character as I have seen cosplayers with no commitment whatsoever.

The most important thing, I believe, when choosing a character, is to make sure both the costume and the character themselves are in your personality wheelhouse. If you're an introvert who's not super comfortable around crowds or being the center of attention, maybe Deadpool – who is anything but that – might not be the best character for you in order to get the feedback you desire. That said, plenty of characters have alternate versions of them (especially in comic books), and a little research can potentially bring up a different version of a character that would be better suited for your personality.

To make your character believable, if that's what you want to do, you have to do your homework and know what they like and don't like, their catchphrases, and so on. A good example of this: a friend of mine cosplays Black Bolt, a member of the Inhumans, who is known for remaining mostly silent as his voice triggers massively destructive shockwaves. So, when he's in costume, he won't say a single word, and if he needs to talk he's sure to remove the mask to mentally break that fourth wall a bit. This might seem small and insignificant to some, but to many it's a total commitment to the character.

The devil is in the detail when it comes to your character, and the very same way that you seek out research material for the character's appearance and costume itself can be used for learning their mannerisms. Your main ingredient when deciding how to cosplay a character should be finding what about that character works within your personality, and if there are any aspects about them that would require you to step out of your comfort zone. With so many tools at our fingertips these days, thanks to technology, we have the opportunity to look beyond the pages of a comic book and, along with our imagination, shape and mold our character into the ideal representation of who we want them to be.

LIGHTS! CAMERA! ACTION!

The Overstreet® Guide To Collecting Movie Posters
takes our "How To" series to the cinema to explore the history and artistry
of movie posters, old and new, American and foreign, across the genres of
horror, Disney, adventure, comedy and many more...

Full color, filled with plenty of visual examples
and all the basics of grading, preservation and storage.

www.gemstonepub.com

THE INS AND OUTS OF CONVENTION WEAPONS POLICIES

By Eddie Newsome

Many weapons can't be carried around out and about in public areas – meaning many weapons can't be carried out and about at conventions, either. As many popular characters tend to have distinctive weapons, it's exceedingly important to pay attention to a con's weapons policy before donning your mask and heading to the event.

While every convention is different, most of the things that are common across the board can be seen below; banned weapons usually include:

• Functional firearms (this also includes air soft guns, BB guns, cap guns, paintball guns and pellet guns)

• Realistic replica firearms (reproductions, fake or toy guns that can be confused for functional firearms)

• Sharpened metal-bladed weapons (swords, daggers, axes, throwing stars and knives, etc.)

• Functional projectile weapons (crossbows, long bows, short bows, slingshots, etc.)

• Explosives (including firecrackers and fireworks)

• Chemical weapons

• Blunt weapons (brass knuckles, hockey sticks, clubs, nunchaku, baseball bats)

• Hard prop weapons (metal, fiberglass, etc.)

• Anything that could, whether accidentally or purposefully, cause injury to another attendee

• All costume weapons must conform to state and federal law.

• Projectile costume weapons

Prop guns look great in photos but might not be allowed on the convention floor.

must be rendered inoperable.

As a rule of thumb, metal weapons – especially "live steel" – are almost always a no-no. As for guns, if it started out as a toy, chances are you'll be good; painted and re-purposed Nerf guns have become popular at conventions as props for this exact reason. Most fake guns that have that distinctive orange tip on them are going to be fine at most conventions, but some conventions have started banning any weapon

Rocket's gun might look intimidating, but it was made out of foam and plastic, making it a great and impressive show-floor prop.

An assassin's blade might do harm in a virtual world, but at a convention, it's best to make sure that it's made out of plastic!

that was ever able to fire a projectile. This would rule out even a lot of toy guns.

With the rise in usage of foam, Worbla, 3D-printing and other alternative means of prop-making, it's now easier than ever to work within the constraints that these rules create. That said, just because something is made out of foam, it doesn't mean that you won't be stopped and asked to put it away. Popular video game and anime characters have often had larger-than-life swords, and carrying around a six-foot-long chunk of foam and Worbla can cause problems if you're in a crowded convention hall. It's just as important to pay attention to a size restriction in a weapons policy as it is to pay attention to what materials you choose to make the weapon.

Many conventions require that prop weapons be checked in and tagged during the registration process. While no one wants to take pictures with a big neon green tag on their fabulous prop, most conventions take place in generally public areas, and these tags help the non-attendees in the area feel safer about what's happening.

Ultimately, just be sure that before you get to work on your next big prop project that you check the weapons policy of whatever convention you're planning on attending. By familiarizing yourself with these policies and the standard banned props within them, you – and your fellow cosplayers and convention attendees – will have a smoother, more fun convention experience.

SITUATIONAL AWARENESS AT CONVENTIONS

By Carrie Wood

Knowing where you are at a convention is one of the most important things to keep in mind. And I don't simply mean asking yourself "Where am I in relation to the artist alley?" I'm talking about putting yourself in the bigger picture of the area – *situational awareness*.

Most conventions that cosplayers regularly appear at – sci-fi, comics, anime, video games, and so on – tend to draw a lot of attention to themselves. A lot of that attention is focused on the cosplayers themselves, because they look so out of the ordinary compared to the regular setting. What this means, though, is that cosplayers need to be aware of the kind of image that they're giving off to the general public while they're at a convention, and need to do what they can in order to avoid raising concerns. In particular, this means paying a lot of attention to the kind of prop they're carrying around with them. Sometimes, cosplayers are going to be asked to leave certain things at home, or otherwise have to go through a lengthy security check.

I was in Boston for an anime convention just a couple of weeks after the bombing at the Boston Marathon occurred. While I had attended this convention previously, I had never seen any sort of security presence like this at a nerd-fest in all of my years of cosplaying up until that point. Not only were there fully-armed security personnel patrolling the convention grounds, but just the process of getting into the building became an event. Full bag checks, bomb-sniffing dogs, metal detectors, pat-downs – the whole shebang. It meant that getting into the convention took significantly longer than what people were used to, and with lines moving slowly, fellow cosplayers began to complain. *Loudly*.

Most of us in the line couldn't believe that anyone would complain about the heightened security measures – the bombing took place just blocks from where the convention was being held, and the con was likely the biggest event to take place in the city since the Marathon happened. Of course the security would be maxed out. And, in the grand scheme of things, it was a pretty minor inconvenience for us at the convention for the city at large to feel safer about the goings-on.

In fact, most big conventions in big cities are going to have a bigger security presence than smaller events in smaller towns, simply because of the greater risk of something terrible happening. It's just something to keep in mind; if you're carrying around a prop gun in a big metropolitan area, expect to be stopped by a police officer at some point.

However, even some small conventions can have tight security depending on the location. I used to help run cosplay events for my university's anime convention, which was run by the anime club on campus. Because the convention was located in the student union, smack dab in the middle of a huge university campus, we had to stick to the university's rules regarding prop weapons: none allowed, at all. A lot of cosplayers were pretty peeved with us about this rule, which, as a cosplayer myself, I can understand. If I spent a ton of time on a prop to go with a costume for a convention and then was told I couldn't bring it with me, I'd be mad about that, too. But at the same time, if a kid who lives on campus sees a cosplayer with a prop gun and mistakes it for a real one, calls the cops and then the whole campus ends up on lockdown… that probably means "no more convention."

What all of this means, though, is that sometimes there are more important things than being able to carry around your prop at a convention the way you want to. Cosplay is a ton of fun, but can sometimes be startling to the people who live and work in the cities where conventions take place. At the end of the day, it's important to realize that the comfort of the general public is more important than your hobby. There will always be another opportunity for some great photos of you and your prop.

How to Pack and Travel for Conventions

One of the most important pre-con preparations (besides finishing your costumes) is properly packing for the show. Be it by air or by car, packing can be one of the most detail-oriented things you can deal with when it comes to prep work, so here's just a few tips and tricks to help out.

1. If you are flying to your destination, keep in mind that if you have toiletries in your carry-on, the allowed amount is 3.4 ounces – which is now basically the standard for "travel sized" items that can be purchased at most stores (see image #1). The only exceptions to this are baby formula, prescription drugs, or over-the-counter medications, which should be kept in a sealed plastic bag in your carry-on for TSA inspection.

2. If your suitcase has compartments inside, this would be the ideal place to store wigs and accessories for your costume (see images #2). Since this is usually a zippered-off section, it provides a safe space to put it for travel plus keeps small items like jewelry and small accessories in one designated area.

3. When possible, especially if your suitcase allows for a divider, it's a good idea to keep your costume items and regular everyday clothing separated to allow for easier unpacking and storage once you reach your destination (see image #3).

4. Be aware of the weight and size of your bags for both carry-on luggage and check-in luggage. Carry-on luggage usually maxes out at about 45 inches in height, though it differs from airline to airline; check-in luggage usually maxes out at 50 pounds per piece, and fees can get up to the $60 range for anything over that limit.

5. With each of your costumes, have a checklist of everything that goes with it; this might be something to consider making as you actually work on your costume, when it's freshest on your mind! Checklists in general are your best friend when it comes to packing for a convention.

1 Travel-sized toiletries ready for TSA inspection

Speaking of checklists, here's ours in regards to the must-haves for convention travel:

Clothing:

- Comfortable pants or shorts
- Comfortable shoes
- Underwear
- Shoe insoles to make those long lines more bearable
- Club/formal wear if you frequent convention dances or after-parties

Toiletries/Personal Hygiene:

- Body wash
- Toothbrush and toothpaste
- Mouthwash
- Hand sanitizer
- Deodorant
- Razors, shaving cream, or whatever other method you prefer for hair removal

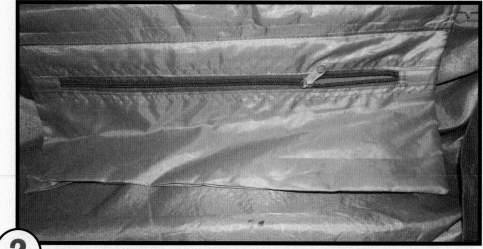

2 Zippered compartment ideal for wigs and accessories

Toiletries/Personal Hygiene (continued):

- Shampoo and conditioner
- Feminine products
- Over-the-counter pain or allergy medications
- Any other medications you might be taking
- Make-up
- Contacts or glasses if needed for daily or costume use

Various other miscellaneous important things:

- Driver's license or other official ID card
- Cash or credit/debit cards
- Business cards
- Hotel information and con badge or confirmation
- Phone charger
- Portable external phone battery for at-con usage
- Batteries
- Extension cord or power strip
- Camera

3 The divider keeping your costume items and regular everyday clothing separated

Cosplay-specific items:

- Your costume (make a separate checklist for each outfit you bring)
- Wig head and wig styling tools
- Odor eliminator spray (such as Febreze)
- Hot glue gun with glue sticks
- Cosplay emergency kit - see our separate article in the book about what this should contain

Our last tip for once you're checked in to your hotel is: *unpack as soon as possible*! Double-check that you have everything on your list as you unpack, and try to get as much of your stuff hung up and put away neatly. As many people arrive to convention hotels the night before the show actually starts, that's a great opportunity to identify any missing or broken pieces and get to a nearby store to replace or fix them. Keep our tips and lists in mind and you're sure to have an easy time with cosplay travel!

HOW TO PUT TOGETHER YOUR COSPLAY EMERGENCY KIT

Anything can happen at a convention, especially if you happen to be wearing an unwieldy costume around on the show floor. While many conventions have begun to feature cosplay repair stations (which is unbelievably considerate of them), many don't have the space for such a luxury. As a cosplayer, you should be prepared for the worst-case scenario in regards to your outfit that you probably spent a lot of time and money on.

If you're staying in a hotel by the convention, you might be able to bring more in terms of cosplay repair items – we've known people who have brought their entire sewing machine setup to the con with them just in case something *drastic* happened, but they almost never needed to use it. (*Almost* being the key word there.) However, for many others at a convention, just having the necessities on them can be a huge help.

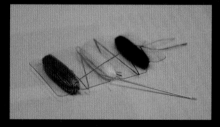

Here is a list of the sort of things that you should bring with you to a convention in case of an emergency – specifically, things that are easily packed into a small pouch as to not take up too much bag space.

ABSOLUTE NECESSITIES:

Super glue: You can get teeny-tiny, individual-use sized super glue just about anywhere these days. Did something fall off or break? Ta-da, you can fix it on the spot. Be sure to get the kind that sets fairly quickly, instead of the stuff that takes a few hours – because otherwise, what's the point?

Safety pins: Did something rip? Pin it back together!

Detergent pen: Spills and slips happen, and sometimes you end up with cola on your dress or ketchup on your tunic. If it's not a big spill, but a noticeable one, a quick rub from a detergent pen can be a huge help in removing the stain.

Deodorant: To prevent the dreaded con funk, clearly. Even if you applied before you left your hotel room, walking around a convention for a few hours will remove most of that freshness. A tiny travel-sized stick or roller is a great option to have.

Hand sanitizer: Just to help ward off the post-convention crud. This is another item that comes in small travel sizes and won't take up much room in your bag.

Bandages: Because cosplay shoes are often uncomfortable and unrealistic and you will someday trip and bust your knee open. Trust us.

Water: Stay hydrated!

OPTIONAL DEPENDING ON THE COSTUME:

Needle and thread: If your costume is primarily fabric-based, this is pretty important! Be sure to bring small spools of thread that match the color of your costume, and if anything rips, you can sew that sucker right up. Alternatively, just get one of those tiny travel sewing kits if you have the room for it.

Straight pins: In case of big tears, these will help a bit in the repair process.

Scissors: For snipping that thread, or perhaps for a quick wig trim. Tiny scissors are super easy to find, too, and often come pre-packed in existing travel-sized sewing kits.

Bobby pins: For keeping stray hairs in the wig cap and to prevent the wig from sliding around on your head.

Fashion tape: Be sure to get the double-sided stuff if you can. Physics and gravity are some pretty significant forces that often work against costumes, and this stuff can help in a pinch when it comes to keeping stockings up or some of the more delicate areas covered.

Makeup: This depends a lot on how much makeup you're using, but having some foundation and eyeliner available for touchups throughout the day is generally a good thing to have. For more serious makeup jobs like body paint, having some additional paint in your bag is probably a good idea, too.

Eye drops: For those who are wearing costume contacts with their cosplay, having drops on hand is a lifesaver for if the contacts get a little uncomfortable during the day.

Cosplayer Spotlight: Bluucircles

First off, please introduce yourself!
Bluucircles: My name is Amanda, and I go by Bluucircles. I've been cosplaying since 2003. I'm from New York, born and raised my whole life, and I currently live in Brooklyn.

What was your first introduction to the cosplay hobby? What was it about cosplay that made you want to participate?
Bluucircles: I recall around 2002 was when I started to become more aware of conventions and cosplaying. I started to get a feeling when I saw a character in a show or movie or game that I liked and thought, "wow, I really want to be them!" With cosplaying, I could not only show my love for a character, but explore my creative outlets as well, in addition to befriending others who also had the same interests.

What is your personal approach to your costumes? How do you choose what character to emulate? Do you tend to make your own outfits, or do you receive help?
Bluucircles: I find I am usually drawn to fun and upbeat characters, with personalities either similar to myself, or with traits I wish I could add (usually characters are a bit more bold and daring than I am in

real life). Other times, it is a fantastic character design that will make me go "wow, that needs to be on my body immediately."

While I make my costumes entirely myself, I will of course seek advice from friends when faced with a perplexing issue that I think they may have a solution for. I can't tell you how many times I've had my butt saved. Of course, they do the same with me. That's one of the things I love about cosplaying with friends, too: it's this giant wealth of knowledge that we all share from and draw from.

What challenges or issues do you think cosplayers face most?
Bluucircles: I think a lot of the time we are seen as not being "normal." I recall one time on the news, the reporters were outside of the Javits on the Friday of New York Comic Con. The reporters kept saying things like, "don't you have jobs?" and it really angered me. We are people, just like anyone else who have jobs, family and a life. And just like anyone else would, we also can take vacations and do what we would like on our days off. Something that really struck a nerve with me and is probably one of my biggest frustrations is society's view of cosplayers.

Of course, I could go on about the cosplay not being consent issue too, as that is certainly another huge one. But we'd be here forever then.

How do you think cosplay adds to the overall convention experience?
Bluucircles: As a cosplayer, it gives me a way to get together with my friends to make memories, to gather together to indulge in something we like, from a series that we like, and to laugh and make a unique experience that can't be replicated. As a spectator, I think it's always fascinating to see what people have been working on, what they've poured all their time and love in.

Any final thoughts?
Bluucircles: Cosplay is an ever-changing and ever-growing thing. I've been cosplaying for more than a decade now and I'm always learning something new. It is a hobby that has introduced me to so many friends, new interests, and new places. It is something I'm deeply happy to be part of.

Photo credit:
Felicis Rook

VIRGINIA COMICON

RICHMOND, VA

It might not be the overwhelming experience of a New York or San Diego, but this Richmond-based convention certainly packs a lot into two short days. With a number of convention exclusives separating the show from the pack, the Virginia Comicon has been able to stay true to the classic convention scene without feeling stale. Retailers from all over the region seem to flock to this show, which also features appearances from popular cosplayers, creators, and various other media guests.

Virginia Comicon
– Richmond, VA

Held during the fall at the
Richmond Raceway Complex.

What cosplay-specific events are offered?

There is a large costume contest
that brings out some top-notch
costumes across ages and genres
due to the fact that there are so
many categories to enter in. The
show also brings in a number of
popular cosplayers as guests for
the weekend, and the programming
schedule also features a number of
panels focused on the hobby.

How do these events impact the convention at large?

When the costume contest gets
started, the focus is generally on
that – there is a noticeable drop
in the amount of feet on the show
floor. Because of how the show is
laid out, it's nigh-impossible to not
notice the huge cosplayer presence.

PROS AND CONS OF THE REGION

Pros: Richmond is the capital of Virginia, so there's a number of major routes into the area, making it an easy travel destination for anyone not local to the region, and the fact that the Raceway Complex offers free parking is another major upside to this show.

Cons: There isn't much at the convention complex beyond the show itself, and there isn't a whole lot within walking distance, either; someone in your con-going party better have a car, otherwise you're stuck with the limited and some-what-pricey con center food.

OTHER THINGS TO DO IN THE REGION

1. Richmond is a richly historic town, having played a major role in both the Revolutionary War and the Civil War. A number of monuments and museums can be found around the city, such as the American Civil War Center and the Richmond National Battlefield Park, so it's a great opportunity for history buffs to explore.

2. Despite its size, Richmond doesn't have any major professional sports teams (though it does have clubs in both USL Soccer and in Double-A Baseball). However, there are two Division I college teams in town: the VCU Rams and the Richmond Spiders, the former of which made a Final Four appearance in 2011.

COSPLAY SHOWCASE
VIRGINIA COMICON 2014   SATURDAY

Mason Van Brunt
Hiccup

Nicole Jacobs
Black Adam/Mary Marvel

Christina Perron
Shazam!

Rebecca Hawk
Vocaloid Luka

Ben Green
The Tenth Doctor

Jessica Pye
Lara Croft

Krista & Brandon Betteridge
Star Wars Tusken Raiders

Andrew Blake
The Mad Hatter

Walter Wade & Jennifer Poole
Star-Lord & Gamora

Brandon Williams
Warhammer 40K Space Marine

Christopher Franklin
Kingsguard

Lisa Crenshaw
Ursula

Matt Adams
Megazord

Isabelle Brown
Harley Quinn

Goldie Daniels
Poison Ivy

Dorothy Stilwell
Jubilee

Jerry Stilwell
Sabretooth

Cameron King
Wolverine

Tess Banky & Corey Prosise
Mera & Aquaman

Hex Nottingham
Darth Maul

COSPLAY SHOWCASE
VIRGINIA COMICON 2014 SUNDAY

BRETT COOPER
SPIDER-MAN

RACHEL GESSLEIN
ELDER SCROLLS

KELSEY ERICKSEN
ASUKA LANGLEY SORYU

CHRISTOPHER MACKEY
ZOD

SEAN & ALEX O'CONNELL
GREEN ARROW & SPEEDY

SAMANTHA WILSON
BAD WOLF TARDIS

AMY WHITELAW
MS. MARVEL

RACHEL MYRICK
LITTLE SISTER
FROM BIOSHOCK

BRANDEN MYRICK
BIG DADDY FROM BIOSHOCK

Damacia Johnson
Pinhead

Damion McCloud
Galactus

Jesse Hodges
Rocket Raccoon

Jason Burkett
The Jedi Dude

Jonathan Morris
Jace the Mind Sculptor

Logan Wolk
The Eleventh Doctor

Jessica Pye
Silent Hill Nurse

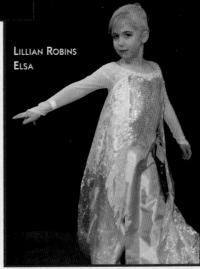

Lillian Robins
Elsa

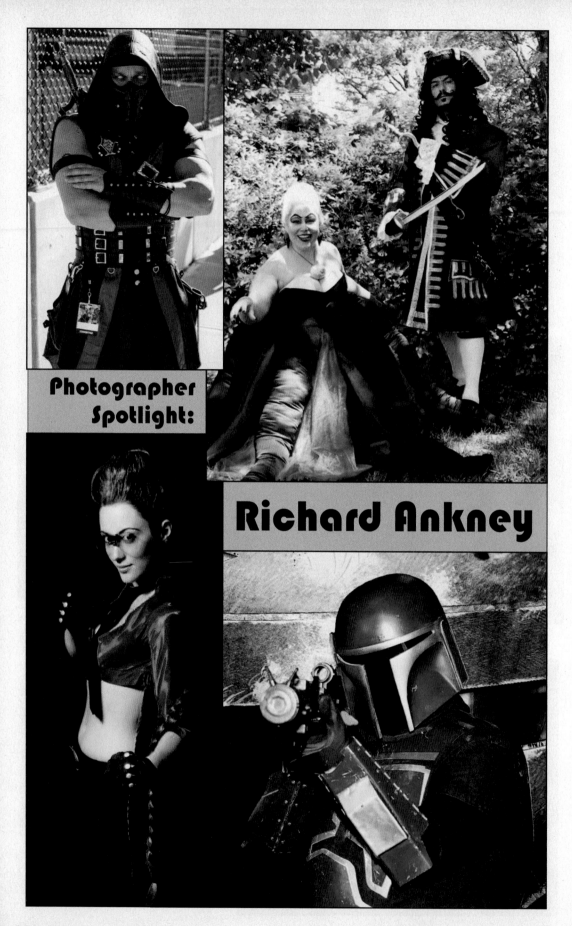

Photographer Spotlight:

Richard Ankney

What did you have an interest in first – photography or cosplay?
Richard Ankney (RA): Cosplay was my first interest, as I have only been doing photography for just over two years now. I have been going to conventions for over 20 years so seeing the cosplayers was always a treat!

What piqued your interest in photography?
RA: Well, I kept seeing so many amazing photos with such great artistic insight that I thought, "Hey, I wanna try that!"

So I started working with some photographers and cosplayers as a visual concept artist and eventually picked up a camera and started shooting.

What do you think differs between cosplay photography and other more "conventional" forms of photography?
RA: I feel that cosplay photography has an inherent level of fun to it. When you get a photographer and cosplayer together who are both obvious fans of the cosplay being done, there is nothing but awesome coming from it. Whereas, while the more convention-oriented photography can be fun, it can also really come across as a job.

What are the biggest challenges that a cosplay photographer tends to face?
RA: I think as a new photographer on the scene, the biggest hurdle is getting people to shoot with you, as there are so many amazing cosplay photographers out there.

But don't be discouraged, as this is a community where a lot of the photographers and cosplayers are all about sharing ideas, experience and just enjoying their fandom.

Would you say there are trends in cosplay photography in the same sense that there are noticeable trends in cosplay itself?
RA: Of course: be it from wanting to use similar equipment, to shooting similar poses, you cannot help but see trends.

A good example is the use of the 85mm lens - many cosplay photographers will say

that is their go-to lens. I feel doing what is trendy isn't a bad thing, because it may be a new style of shooting for you, but don't let it take away from your individual style as well. Always try to stay true to your own art.

Do you have any memorable moments from your time as a cosplay photographer that you'd want to share?
RA: Wow, there are so many! I think that the most memorable things I have experienced so far are those moments when you see a cosplayer online in social media and develop a love for their craft, only to then meet them at a convention and getting to fan out with them over their work - only to hear that they love my work as well!

Those are the moments I love best! Oh… and then getting to shoot with them!

Cosplayer Spotlight: Knightmage

Please introduce yourself!
Knightmage: My name is Michael Wilson, a.k.a. Knightmage. I grew up in Cleveland, Ohio and now reside in Youngstown, Ohio.

What is one of the best or most memorable experiences you've had in cosplay?
Knightmage: This is a really tough question. Every time I suit up it's memorable, and usually it's for different reasons. Going to conventions, it's because I get to see friends and hang out with them, plus have attendees look at and comment on my costumes. It really fills you with pride knowing someone, strangers, really appreciates something that you put together.

When I'm at a charity event, seeing the smiles from kids as they see their favorite superhero and then seeing the smiles from adults as they see their kids smile. All those moments are great and memorable.

What kind of issues do you feel cosplayers face the most these days?
Knightmage: With geek culture and more specifically cosplaying becoming more and more main stream there seems to be a growing competitive approach to it. There's absolutely nothing wrong with competition and wanting to do the best you can, but like all things there can be negative sides to it as well. In this competitive construct, you have those that will bully,

troll, and put others down only because it's the only way to lift themselves up. The sad truth is that there's nothing you can do about these people. They exist, they're out there just waiting to pounce and they're not going anywhere. It can be extremely discouraging. I always tell new cosplayers this. They need to know about the ugly side.

However, there's always an opposite side. With every negative look, every horrible comment, there's hundreds of positive. The cosplay community as a whole is an extremely friendly and supporting community. Sure, there are a few bad apples but you'll have that in any faction or community. Those bad apples don't compare to the amount of good ones. That's where your focus needs to be.

What do you think cosplay adds to the overall convention experience?
Knightmage: Much like sports, fandoms in geek culture bring people together regardless of race, political opinions and anything else. If you're a fan of a character and you see a cosplayer dressed as that character, right there you've formed a small bond. It's a conversation starter. When kids and adults get to see the characters they love walking in front of them. They get to hug them, take a picture and pose with them. It's special. It's an amazing memory they'll have from that convention. Cosplayers are starting to become major show pieces of these conventions. People are coming to see the cosplayers just as much as they're coming to see convention exclusives.

It might not be a popular opinion but cosplayers are becoming celebrities in their own right. Cosplayers are now becoming guests at conventions. People, fans, are coming just to see and talk to these cosplayers. I personally think it's awesome. A lot of people downplay it saying, these people are just dressing up. They're nothing special. I say tell that to the kid who looks up to that cosplayer. The kid who follows them on social media. The kid who is inspired by their words or deeds or creativity. So I think cosplay adds a lot to the overall convention experience.

MEGACON
ORLANDO, FL

What kicked off back in 1993 as a tiny convention held in a mall is now one of the biggest shows in the U.S. The show is now a four-day event that covers comic books, science fiction, anime, video games, horror and more; it's a true pop culture experience. MegaCon fully takes over the Orange County Convention Center with geek-centric activities of all kinds, from gaming to LARP and even film festivals. This is a convention where you can go to a nice photoshoot by a lake, then go to a panel on belly dancing, and then cap it off with an anime-themed dance party – it's truly an overwhelming but awesome experience.

Photos courtesy of
John W. McAdams III and Moana McAdams

MegaCon – Orlando, FL
Held during the spring at the Orange County Convention Center.

What cosplay-specific events are offered?
The cosplay masquerade is the highlight of costume-focused fare at MegaCon, but there's also panels and workshops that cover the topic as well. Panels have in the past also included cosplay game shows as well as cosplay "speed dating," which helps to create a unique mix of entertainment.

How do these events impact the convention at large?
Cosplayers are everywhere and you're unlikely to get down a hallway without getting stopped for a photo (or wanting to take someone else's)! But with so much going on, it's almost a non-issue for non-cosplayers.

PROS AND CONS OF THE REGION

Pros: Because Orlando is such a popular vacation destination, it's easy to find affordable flights into the city, and MegaCon's location puts it around plenty of hotels that offer shuttle services to the show; there's also a number of wonderful photoshoot locations around the center for cosplayers to take advantage of.

Cons: The heat is definitely an issue in Florida, and with the con's date having been steadily inching ever closer to the summer, it's a huge factor in terms of what costume to bring to the show and what others to leave in the closet.

OTHER THINGS TO DO OUTSIDE OF MegaCon

1. As mentioned, it's a big vacation destination – for big reasons! Whether you prefer Disney or Universal, the theme parks and resorts are not far away and can turn a quick con weekend into a longer family outing.

2. For those who enjoy the nightlife, there are a lot of geek-themed parties that take place after con hours in the area around MegaCon, making for a really nice tie-in to the rest of your congoing experience.

EMERALD CITY COMICON

SEATTLE, WA

PACIFIC NORTHWEST

The gem of the northwestern convention scene, Emerald City Comicon, first kicked off in 2003 as a one-day event. Now, ECCC draws tens of thousands of people to the Washington State Convention and Trade Center by bringing in a number of guests from the comic industry and elsewhere in entertainment – plus a massive exhibition floor and a variety of other events. Show exclusives keep the fans coming year after year and, of course, there's plenty for cosplayers to do at the show as well.

Photos courtesy of
John W. McAdams III and Moana McAdams

Emerald City Comicon – Seattle, WA

Held every spring at the Washington State Convention Center

What cosplay-specific events are offered?

They've got panels and workshops related to costuming, plus a big costume contest that features a number of categories for costumes from science fiction, fantasy, video game, comic books, and more.

How do these events impact the show at large?

ECCC is a huge con and cosplayers often want to make a splash with a costume there, so you're bound to see some truly impressive work – but there's so much to do at such a large show that it's easy to skip over the cosplay-centric events.

Disability services: ECCC, like New York Comic Con, operates under ReedPOP and follows the same Medical Assistance program. Attendees can reserve a Medical Sticker by applying in advance of the con; the sticker alerts staff to the person wearing it and their additional needs and also allows the bearer to access special queue lines and other benefits. Service animals are also allowed and the convention has a limited space available for those who need to keep medications stored in a cold environment.

PROS AND CONS OF THE REGION

Pros: You're in Seattle, a major city, so it's pretty easy to get to by plane or otherwise, plus as an urban area there's lots to do outside the convention center.

Cons: The northwest in early spring can be quite chilly, so much like going to a southern convention in the summer, it's crucial to plan appropriate outfits in order to have the most comfortable time.

OTHER THINGS TO DO IN THE REGION

1. There's an exciting night life that surrounds ECCC, with several convention-themed parties taking place on every night of the show, so there's no reason to turn in early!

2. Science fiction fans can visit the EMP Museum, home to the Science Fiction Museum and Hall of Fame, which contains memorabilia related to **Star Trek, Lost in Space, Star Wars** and more; music fans can find a lot at the EMP Museum too, as Seattle is the birthplace of Jimi Hendrix, and the museum highlights photographs and personal instruments of the legendary guitarist.

Cosplayer Spotlight: Tonia Antilla

Photographs provided by Tonia Antilla

What first got you interested in cosplay?
Tonia Antilla (TA): Well, I've always loved theater and grew up around it. I am also a life-long artist of many mediums. So when I was invited to participate in my first comic con I had to go in costume. I made one myself, by hand as I did not own a working sewing machine at that time. I went to my first con in my first cosplay and had an absolute blast. It was magical being able to be the character and have others play along with me.

What's your personal approach to the hobby?
TA: I approach with my heart first. I love people and interacting with people. I love making them smile. If joy comes from your heart, it is

contagious and will impact others. I enjoy making cons fun for everyone. I also use cosplay as "cause-play." There is a whole community out there who uses their cosplay talents for charity. We raise money for Make-a-Wish, children's hospitals, prosthetics and wigs for children, playrooms for non-profit children's hospitals, walks for cancer, you name it. This makes it personal for me, and joyful.

How do you pick a character to emulate?
TA: Usually I pick a character for the sheer challenge of creating the cosplay. Sometimes it is a character that is rarely seen or an unusual cosplay. Sometimes I see a movie costume and just challenge myself to recreate it. I usually stick to *Star Wars*; I'm a *huge Star Wars* geek!

Do you tend to make your costumes yourself?

TA: I do make the costumes myself. I don't (or haven't yet) commission pieces out for my cosplays. I make patterns, sew, sculpt, cast, and I work with leather, prosthetics, plastics, and just about anything except metal.

What are your strengths and weaknesses in regards to costume construction?

TA: I think in pictures! I can take things apart and put them back together and rotate them in my head, so figuring out how things are put together and how materials are going to work together is usually pretty easy. I'm also very tenacious and don't give up very easily at all if at all - I make it work one way or another. As far as weaknesses, I'm terrible about testing things out or doing test areas with textiles, paints and dyes. I just want to do it and roll the dice. So far I have been pretty lucky. I also hate waiting for molds to cure, castings to cure, dyes and paints to dry - I want it all done now!

There are obviously lots of great experiences to be had in cosplay, but can you think of any negatives?

TA: Oh boy! Now we just *had* to go there! (Just kidding!) I have had a bad experience and unfortunately it is becoming all too common in the cosplay community. People who want to cosplay will often try to get cosplayers to make them a cosplay, and that's fine, until they steal credit for the creation of the commission and steer business away from the artist. This is a very big no-no and will get a person blacklisted from the community fast. These people are

often re-casters - they steal the artist's work by having molds made of the work and sell castings.

What challenges or issues do you think cosplayers face the most?

TA: Safety is one issue. People sometimes think that female cosplayers are putting themselves out there for physical attention — *not* true. Keeping dignity in the art is another one. No one is better than anyone else. All cosplayers should be treated with respect by their peers. And of course, cosplay is not consent. Please treat cosplayers with dignity and respect, and we will show you that in return.

Do you think cosplay adds to the overall convention experience?

TA: I absolutely do! A great majority of people who attend cons want to see the cosplayers. It is also free advertisement for pop culture. A con without cosplayers would be like going to Disneyland and never seeing Mickey Mouse!

HEROESCON

CHARLOTTE, NC

SOUTHEAST REGION

The south has found a foothold in the convention scene, with such shows as MegaCon, Florida Supercon, Anime Weekend Atlanta, and Dragon Con all having become big draws for cosplayers from around the country. A mainstay in this region though is definitely Heroes Convention, or simply HeroesCon, which has been held every year since 1982. But even before that, showrunner Shelton Drum had been running Charlotte Mini-Con.

"A couple of years in I felt it was time to make something bigger out of it," Drum said. "So in 1982 I decided to do a bigger show, and over the years it's taken on a life of its own. We try to focus only on comics and comic creators, and we've continued to do that, and that's where we've made our niche."

HeroesCon - Charlotte, NC
Held in the summer at the Charlotte Convention Center, located in downtown Charlotte.

What cosplay specific events are offered?
A cosplay group photo known as "The Class Picture," as well a costume contest that offers prizes in different age and group categories. You can also usually find cosplay-focused panels amongst the programming schedule at the show.

What impact do these events have on the convention at large?
The Class Photo is a big draw of the cosplay aspect of the convention, but as there isn't a huge focus on costuming beyond that and the contest, it's up to the attendee to decide whether or not it will be a big part of the show.

Disability Services: Services are offered that provide a safe and secure environment as well as reserved seating, plus service dog compliance.

PROS AND CONS OF THE REGION

Pros: Located in the heart of downtown Charlotte, making it very easy to get to via public transportation for those staying elsewhere in the city area.

Cons: There isn't a shuttle service provided from hotels to the show, and the fact that this is a summer con held in the south should speak for itself – those in heavy costumes will get uncomfortably warm uncomfortably fast.

WHAT TO DO IN THE AREA

1. Racing fans will find plenty to enjoy in Charlotte, as the NASCAR Hall of Fame is located in the city. The four floors of the Hall contain a theater, a "Heritage Speedway" that details the history of NASCAR, as well as the Hall of Honor itself.

2. Comic books are sequential art, and fans of art in general can spend some time at the Bechtler Museum of Modern Art. The museum contains works from French, British and American artists, among others, and features primarily 20th-century modernist pieces.

Cosplayer Spotlight: Ruby Rinekso

Please introduce yourself!

Ruby Rinekso (RR): My name is Ruby Rinekso. I've been a New Yorker almost all my life, and living in Queens for most of it. Life outside the world of conventions includes my professional life as a graphic designer and my life as a musician. Most recently, I've been a graphic designer for a children's publishing company. For over 15 years, I've played lead guitar in KISSNATION, The KISS Tribute Show performing venues nationally. In my time with the band, we've been fortunate enough to have the official blessings of original KISS members Gene Simmons and Paul Stanley, who have seen us perform, have been incredibly kind to us, and also provided us with great opportunities for the band.

Do you tend to make your own costumes or do you receive help?

RR: It's always a combination of both. I make what I can, and if there's something that I think exceeds my abilities, I seek help among the cosplaying community. Having said that, if I don't make it myself, I'm still usually involved in the building process in some fashion.

What's been one of your best or most memorable experiences in cosplay?

RR: Superman actor Dean Cain facilitating my proposal to my now-wife Jennifer.

Let me briefly explain: At Dragon Con 2012 in Atlanta, during the DC Comics Cosplay Photoshoot, Dean Cain made a surprise appearance to say "hi" to the fans and cosplayers (over 200 people). After addressing the fans he asked Jennifer (dressed as the 1966 TV Batgirl), to approach him, then asked me (as the 1966 TV Batman) to approach him as well. He then pulled out an engagement ring from his pocket and handed it to me as I proceeded to propose to Jennifer. This moment, of course, was all planned without Jennifer knowing. Photographers and press was there. CNN and *USA Today* reported on it. The moment can be seen on video on YouTube. Last I checked it was over 60K hits. Who knew my proposal would be that popular?

Although Dean could not make the wedding, he did send us a personal video congratulating us. How can I top that moment in cosplaying?

What do you think cosplay adds to the overall convention experience?

RR: I think cosplaying brings life and color to the convention experience. It's part of the show. We bring smiles to children and adults of all ages. Whether there's a cosplayer in a new trendy costume, or a retro and vintage character... there's something for everyone to enjoy, and take photos with.

I believe without cosplayers, all you would have are tables selling merchandise or celebrity photo ops, then it just becomes a flea market, just another shopping expo, another avenue to spend money. What's the fun in that?

Comic-Con International

SAN DIEGO, CA

WEST COAST

In the five days that this convention covers it's impossible to see everything, but that doesn't mean people don't try! Panels covering everything from toy collecting, to how to get published in comics, to steampunk style can be seen, and the vast array of attendees seen rightfully reflects all that SDCC has to offer.

This convention truly encompasses what cons are - that is, if you don't mind waiting in long lines, crowds and the dreaded Hall H. But all of these, for better or worse, are part of the SDCC experience. It's a chance to meet artists, writers and comic book companies that have helped shape and made an impact on fandom at large. While most conventions have the convention center as ground zero, SDCC is the exception to the rule. There are plenty of big shows and companies that have a presence not only inside, but outside the con center as well, with hands on demos of upcoming games, interactive obstacle courses and meet-and-greets. This is the smorgasbord of fandom, the buffet of nerdom and the grab bag of geek that is Comic Con. What was once a small comic book convention has become the definitive pop culture con and that's not a bad thing!

Comic-Con International: San Diego, CA

Held in the summer at the San Diego Convention Center.

What cosplay-specific events are offered?

The masquerade competition is held every year and is definitely one of the marquee events of this show. Cosplayers bring out their best stuff to try and win the big trophy, plus, prizes from companies such as Marvel and Sideshow Collectables have been awarded in the past as well.

What impact do these events have on the convention at large?

Cosplay is not only embraced, it's celebrated, with backdrops everywhere around the convention floor specifically for cosplayers to use for photos. Several of the bigger booths will also host their own costume contests, making SDCC a common place to see some of the biggest and most impressive costumes of the year.

Disability Services: SDCC has always listened and every year improved on their disability services. They provide a rest area for the disabled, the elderly, expectant mothers and parents with small children, a separate registration service for attendees with mobility issues, wheelchairs for loan, ASL interpreters at large panels and events, and special limited seating for certain programming events.

PROS AND CONS OF THE SAN DIEGO REGION

Pros: SDCC is in the heart of the city, making it very easy to get to. Shuttle services are provided as well as free car services by sponsoring companies (if you can spot one). Plus, it's SDCC – that's almost a pro all on its own!

Cons: Parking is a nightmare and can be prohibitively expensive for those trying to park close to the convention center, and just getting passes to the con can be difficult as they sell out quickly.

OTHER THINGS TO DO OUTSIDE THE CON

1. LEGOLAND is a San Diego landmark that offers family fun and a trip that you'll never forget! With plenty of rides to provide entertainment regardless of age, plus a water park, this is definitely worth including as part of the San Diego experience at large.

2. The San Diego Zoo is a worldwide attraction that will educate as well as entertain. The zoo is home to more than 650 species, totaling more than 3,700 animals, and features exhibits that showcase popular attractions such as the gorillas, tigers, and pandas. The San Diego Zoo is one of just four Zoos in the States that have giant pandas, so be sure to stop by!

Cosplayer Spotlight: Eric Moran

What first got you interested in cosplay?

Eric Moran (EM): I was a big fan of comics, sci-fi, horror, et cetera, and I was cosplaying before it was even called cosplay — it was just called costuming. So cosplay became a natural fit.

What was it about cosplay that made you want to participate?

EM: I love cosplaying to meet great people and to create amazing and incredible friendships. I love having met this creative group of people, and they also inspire me to cosplay even better.

What's your personal approach to the hobby? How do you pick a character to emulate?

EM: I just like cosplaying characters I like - there's no real specific approach. I just pick characters that people will be blown away by. And at the same time, I feel I can cosplay anyone, so the world of costuming is very open to me.

Do you tend to make your costumes yourself? What are your strengths and weaknesses in regards to costume construction?

EM: There are some costumes I've made on my own, but I have others from costume and prop makers. These usually lay out the foundation for a costume, like a raw kit for a suit of armor, and then I go in and add my own style, from detailing, to making props to the costumes as add-ons.

Sometimes, I will work on a costume and take a break, and I won't get back to it for a month to a year due to the complexity of it. I have a great wife and friends that motivate me not to give up, though, which is where I draw my strength from.

What do you think cosplay adds to the overall convention experience?

EM: I've said this before and I stand by it, but cosplayers are the *superstars* of comic-cons. When you see picture highlights of conventions now, a good 80 percent of those are the cosplayers, and that's because people want to see who wore the biggest, craziest costume at these events. That's not to take away anything from the artists, vendors, or celebrities. Cosplay is just the new driving force for comic cons of today.

Any final thoughts you'd like to share?

EM: Never limit yourself in cosplay, always thank your photographers, and always be humble and try to inspire others. I also want to thank my wife for not only cosplaying with me, but also always keeping me motivated.

COLOSSALCON

SANDUSKY, OH

All photos by Carrie Wood

While the Midwest has an incredible amount of conventions to attend, one that cosplayers from all over tend to flock to is Colossalcon. This likely has a lot to do with the location; the show is held at the Kalahari Resort and Convention Center, which features a massive indoor/outdoor waterpark, a safari park, and tons of other fun activities to do right on-site. Many cosplayers opt to make convention-specific outfits, such as swimsuits based on popular characters, just to wear in the water at Colossalcon. It's not often that you get to see people putting on wigs just to jump in the water, but if this show proves anything, it's that cosplayers can have just as much fun (if not more) as anyone else at a water park!

Of course, the convention itself always has plenty to offer. With big-name guests, concerts, an artist alley and dealer hall, plus – of course – cosplay contests, Colossalcon has everything attendees have come to expect from an anime convention. The unique venue just puts it over the top, making Colossalcon our Midwest convention of choice!

Colossalcon – Sandusky, OH
Held during the summer at the Kalahari Resort and Conference Center.

What cosplay-specific events are offered?
A masquerade, a fashion show, cosplay chess – standard fare, and nothing out of the ordinary.

What impact do these events have on the convention at large?
For competitive cosplayers, it's a big part of the con, but for everyone else, it's easily avoided. It really depends on how you plan out your convention!

Disability Services: Those needing assistance can check-in with convention security to receive a special addition to their convention badge, granting special seating at events; service animals are also permitted in compliance with Ohio state laws.

Photo?
Sure!
Go ahead

PROS AND CONS OF THE REGION

Pros: Very easy to get to by main highways from a number of different parts of the country, is generally not unbearably hot during the summer
Cons: If you didn't drive to the convention yourself, you're kind of stuck at the Kalahari, since it's not in a particularly densely populated area.

OTHER THINGS TO DO IN THE AREA OUTSIDE OF COLOSSALCON

1. Spend time at the water park itself! The Kalahari is a wonderful and unique venue for a convention, and with most of the water slides actually being indoors, if the weather gets sour there's plenty of indoor fun to be had. Plus, with a Safari Park and rope climbing course, there's plenty of adventure to be had right on-site!

2. Head out to Cedar Point, also located in Sandusky and the second-oldest amusement park in the United States, which is also known as "America's Roller Coast." It's got an incredible 16 roller coasters (and counting) among its world-record 72 rides!

3. Sandusky is located right by the shores of Lake Erie, providing lots of opportunities for swimming, kayaking and lots of other water sports – just be sure to watch out for Bessie!

CONVENTIONS
THE MID-ATLANTIC REGION

Between Baltimore, MD, and Washington, DC, there's an absolute ton of conventions to attend no matter what your specific interests are. Comic books? Check. Anime and manga? Definitely. Video games? Of course!

Baltimore has been home to Otakon, the east coast's largest anime convention, for more than 20 years (though the convention is set to move to DC starting in 2017), plus the Baltimore Comic-Con has been going strong since it kicked off in 2000. Down at the other end of the Baltimore-Washington Parkway, fans can find MAGFest, Katsucon, Awesomecon, Anime USA and much more.

With so many cons taking place in the region throughout the year, there's plenty of cosplay opportunities for those looking to enter their work in competitions or simply just get some good photos. Plus, Baltimore and Washington are both unique cities with plenty of character, making them both excellent destinations for those coming from out of town and looking for something to do outside the convention itself.

PROS AND CONS OF THE REGION

Pros: Generally easy to get to this part of the country whether you're driving, flying, or taking any other mode of transportation, has lots of conventions throughout the year

Cons: Weather in both the winter and summer can be super iffy – winter cons can have two feet of snow potentially dumped on them, and summers can be humid and muggy – so it's important to bring appropriate costumes for the show.

MAGFEST

NATIONAL HARBOR, MD

MAGFest (Music and Gaming Festival) – National Harbor, MD
Main festival held in the winter at the Gaylord National Resort and Convention Center, with smaller fests taking place in Maryland and Virginia through-out the rest of the year.

What cosplay-specific events are offered?
Not a lot! MAGFest isn't super cosplay-focused when it comes to events, though there's usually a small contest and, for those with strong spines, a "roast" is often also held. However, the National Harbor area is super nice for photos, so many cosplayers bring their A-game to this show just for that!

What impact do these events have on the convention at large?
Hardly any! The biggest draw for MAGFest tends to be the four days of gaming across two massive game rooms (one dedicated to arcade cabinets, the other to console gaming), so it tends to be an afterthought as far as convention programming goes.

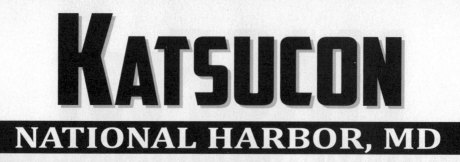

KATSUCON
NATIONAL HARBOR, MD

Katsucon – National Harbor, MD

Held every winter (usually on President's Day Weekend in February) at the Gaylord National Resort and Convention Center.

What cosplay-specific events are offered?

The masquerade continues to be a main event for Katsucon, though the convention also offers a hall costume contest and has also hosted "cosplay chess" as well. You'll also find a number of fan-run panels dealing with the topic of cosplay and costume work.

What impact do these events have on the convention at large?

Katsucon, for many cosplayers, is the convention on the east coast for showing off their best work. Due to the great scenery at National Harbor, it's a popular show for extended private photoshoots, and with the amount of cosplay-focused events, it's impossible to avoid. Cosplay is as big of a focus at Katsucon as just about anything else!

Disability services: Katsucon offers a quick-access registration line for those with accessibility challenges, as well as a badge ribbon that will provide line-jump access, priority seating, and other accommodations. Guests with these requirements much present their ADA card when entering the registration area to be directed to the correct line, and congoers should notify staffers of any additional needs they may have at the show.

AWESOME CON

WASHINGTON, DC

Awesome Con – Washington, DC
Held late spring/early summer at the Walter E. Washington Convention Center

What cosplay-specific events are offered?
The convention holds a big costume contest, but there's no performance aspect of it like you generally see in masquerade contests. Awesome Con also usually gets lots of cosplay guests, many of whom host panels.

What impact do these events have on the convention at large?
Not a lot – if you're a cosplayer, there's plenty for you to do there, but if you're not into that, the events are pretty easily ignored. The show has a ton going for it outside of the cosplay events, making it a good well-rounded event regardless of any interest in cosplay.

Disability services: Awesome Con allows attendees in wheelchairs or crutches to skip lines for autographs, photo ops, and most panels. American Sign Language interpreters are also available at this show on a limited capacity, and those requiring this service to see an info desk for more information at the show. Service animals are also allowed inside the convention center.

OTHER THINGS TO DO IN WASHINGTON, DC

1. It's the nation's capital, so go check out all of the monuments, of course! DC is obviously the place to go for history buffs, and with the metro going all over the area, it's easy to take a couple of hours away from the con and go see the sights!

2. Spend some time bumming around the museums! There's plenty to do at the Smithsonian museums, but there's also some neat things to do at places like the Spy Museum and the Newseum (though unlike the Smithsonian, those aren't free).

OTAKON

Otakon – Baltimore, MD

Held every summer at the Baltimore Convention Center, but scheduled to move to the Walter E. Washington Convention Center in DC beginning in 2017.

What cosplay-specific events are offered?

The masquerade at Otakon has been a marquee event for many years now, and the show also holds a hall costume contest – so, nothing too out of the ordinary. There's also workshops and panels held throughout the weekend by other cosplayers, and Otakon has also provided a huge photo suite for professionally-taken photos against a backdrop for a number of years as well.

What impact do these events have on the convention at large?

Since Otakon is so big and has so much going on, those looking to do something outside of cosplay will be able to find plenty to do. But those cosplayers looking to make it the focus of their weekend can definitely do so as well. Otakon strikes a pretty good balance between cosplay and the rest of the programming. The masquerade has also been held at a different building outside of the convention center in the past, which gives plenty of space to the event without taking up space in the con center.

Disability services: Con-goers that fall into what Otakon refers to as their "Special Needs" category can request assistance and additional services – such as elevator access and priority seating – during the convention. However, Otakon does not provide medical equipment, including wheelchairs, nor do they provide assistance in using such equipment.

Baltimore Comic-Con

BALTIMORE, MD

**Baltimore Comic-Con –
Baltimore, MD**
Held every fall at the Baltimore
Convention Center.

**What cosplay-specific events
are offered?**
The Baltimore Comic-Con
holds an annual costume
contest, usually on Sunday at
the show, with a number of
different categories for entry.
Beyond that, there isn't much
of a focus on cosplay, pro-
gramming-wise.

**What impact do these events
have on the convention at
large?**
Since the contest is held on
the last day of the show,
that's when attendees really
bring out their biggest and
best work when it comes
to costumes. Attendees will
definitely notice the spike in
cosplayers on that last day.
Outside of that, it doesn't
have much of an impact on
the rest of the show, beyond
the cosplayers roaming the
convention space throughout
the weekend.

OTHER THINGS TO DO IN BALTIMORE

1. Check out some of the local attractions in the harbor area, such as the National Aquarium, or take a water taxi out to see historic Fort McHenry!

2. Head to Geppi's Entertainment Museum, conveniently located across the street from the Baltimore Convention Center, for an extra dose of pop culture history!

Cosplayer Spotlight: Aaron Forrester

Please introduce yourself!
Aaron Forrester (AF): My name is Aaron Forrester and I am a Phoenix, Arizona-based costume and prop builder. I am the face behind Aaron's Armory but I am also the founding member of the Arizona Avengers charity costuming club as well as its sister chapters in California, Hawaii and Virginia.

What first got you interested in cosplay?
AF: Although I have been into costumes since I was a child – trick-or-treating on Halloween – it wasn't until about six years ago that I took my talents in doing automotive body and paint work, and applied them to building costumes outside of a Halloween setting. At that time, I was a manager for a local comic book store and after having a visit from my local *Star Wars* costume clubs, I decided right then and there that I wanted to build costumes for fun and for charity.

What is your personal approach to cosplay?
AF: I follow what I like to call as the "Devil's Rule," or the "666 Rule." What this means is that whatever I build, I want it to look good from six yards, six feet, and six inches. Anyone can make a costume that looks good from far away, but as we know, the devil is in the details. Whenever I chose a costume, I try to keep this in mind. Not only do I try to capture the spirit of the character, I aim for accuracy as well.

In regards to how I chose which character I want to portray, I try to stay closer to my body type. Although anyone can cosplay any character, I personally feel more comfortable choosing characters that my body is more similar to. I tend to choose costumes and props that are not typically main stream or popular at that moment in time, which I feel makes them that much more special.

Do you tend to make your costumes yourself? What are your strengths and weaknesses in regards to costume construction?
AF: I typically make costumes and props for myself. On the rare occasion I will take on commissions but I have found that when I do, the stress of a customer's deadlines plus building something that I may not want to build, tends to put a bad taste in my mouth. It makes me not want to work on any projects, including my own. More

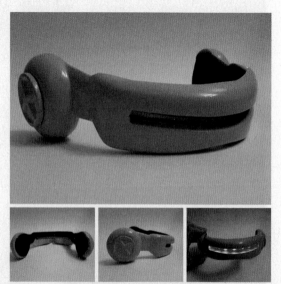

All photos provided by Aaron Forrester

often than not, I'll make something for myself, and others will want one as well. At that point, I'll consider making duplicates for sale. This is my hobby - something I enjoy doing to escape the stresses of work and life. When I turn it into a job, I have therefore lost my hobby and no longer have the fun I once had. That's how it is for me at least.

What challenges or issues do you think cosplayers tend to face the most?

AF: Each individual has their challenges when it comes to this community, but I feel that the most obvious one is how we are viewed in the public eye. Those who are unfamiliar with the hobby tend to have an idea that those involved are very strange for expressing their fandom so passionately and don't understand that it's all about having fun. The media has not helped in this regard either. Rather than spotlight the talents of those who spent weeks, or even months, to accurately portray their character, those individuals are overlooked while attention is focused on the girl who is attractive and wearing a revealing outfit.

I have had family members interested in going to a convention, but were worried about taking their young children as well because what they saw on TV about how women are dressed. I had to explain to them that the majority of people who dress in costume do not dress as the media portray them, but rather are works of art for all

to see and can be nothing short of breathtaking. Although geek culture is much more mainstream than it once was, it still has its stigmas in regular society.

Any final thoughts you'd like to share?

AF: Whether you are new to this hobby or have been involved in it for years, just remember that we all started someplace, and this is about having fun and about sharing our fandoms. Always be willing to help others better their skills so they can in turn help others down the road. This hobby is not about how many fans you have on Facebook, or who looked better in the what costume. At the end of the day, we're just a group of people dressed up in spandex.

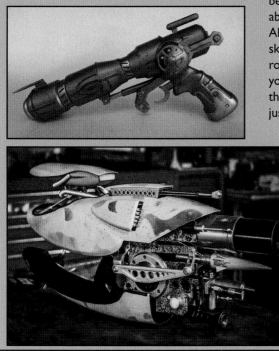

CONVENTIONS
- NEW YORK -

With a city as enormous as New York, it's no surprise that some of the biggest conventions in the United States would take place in the Big Apple! The big draw every fall for the last decade or so has been none other than New York Comic Con, which not only overtakes the Javits Center but also has a number of unique featured events around the city as well. The four-day event always sells out quickly – sometimes within just a couple of hours – and the convention has always delivered on the fan demand just to get in the door. With big-name celebrity guests in addition to the crop of comic writers and artists, NYCC is definitely a must-see, at least once, for pop culture addicts.

For those looking for something a little less insane, there's Eternal Con, held just a short train ride away outside the city limits in Nassau County. A much more toned-down event, Eternal Con takes place over the course of just two days, but boasts a unique venue in the Cradle of Aviation Museum in Garden City, NY.

PROS AND CONS OF THE REGION

Pros: Super easy to get to regardless of your mode of transportation (plane, train, bus, or driving), lots of things to do with your time outside of the convention itself, plus a bounty of unique photoshoot locations for your costumes.

Cons: Staying in New York – particularly in the city – can get pretty expensive, and if you're not a big fan of crowds then this is probably not the area for you.

New York Comic Con

NEW YORK CITY

New York Comic Con – New York, NY
Held during the fall at the Jacob K. Javits Convention Center in Manhattan.

What cosplay-specific events are offered?
A huge costume contest – the Eastern Championships of Cosplay – which offers large cash prizes in addition to acting as the prelim to the "Crown Championships of Cosplay." There's also a ton of panels on the subject offered throughout the weekend, official fan meet-ups for different series, and more.

What impact do these events have on the convention at large?
Cosplayers have a tendency to bring out their absolute best for NYCC as it's one of the largest conventions and therefore one of the best places to get noticed – but the cosplay events themselves don't have a huge impact on the schedule for those looking to do something else.

Disability Services: Fans needing special assistance should apply for a "Medical Assistance Sticker" which will identify them to NYCC staff and security as someone who may need additional assistance. Those with stickers have priority seating for some panels and screenings as available and are able to queue up for events in a separate dedicated space. Please note that the sticker must be applied for in advance; wheelchairs, canes and other mobility devices must also be reserved. For those with anxiety and related problems, a dedicated Quiet Room is available at the show.

OTHER THINGS TO DO OUTSIDE OF NYCC

1. It's a part of New York Super Week, so there's a bevy of events taking place around the city during this time! Whether you're going to an official fan gathering or an after-party, there's plenty of ways to keep the con going outside of the Javits Center.

2. Uh, you're in New York City – there's **always** something to do! Whether you're shopping, visiting the museums or just taking in the sights, there's so much going on that you won't have any trouble killing time while you're in town for the convention.

ETERNAL CON

GARDEN CITY, NY

Eternal Con – Garden City, NY
Held during the summer at the Cradle of Aviation Museum.

What cosplay-specific events are offered?
There's a cosplay contest as one of the marquee events of the show, plus panels and fandom meetups. Cosplay guests are also a staple of the show, and Eternal Con has also been host to a "cosplay parade" at the show.

What impact do these events have on the convention at large?
Cosplay is absolutely a focal point for Eternal Con, so the hobby definitely dominates the convention – but for those not looking to compete, there's a ton of other things to do, such as check out the game rooms, do some shopping, meet the guests and even check out the museum itself.

OTHER THINGS TO DO OUTSIDE OF ETERNAL CON

1. Garden City is home to the immense Roosevelt Field shopping center, which is located directly on top of the former airfield where Charles Lindbergh took off on his famous 1927 transatlantic flight – oh, and it happens to be a solid place to get some shopping in, too.
2. Nassau County is home to a number of different sports teams, some of whom can be potentially caught at home during the weekend of Eternal Con – or, just hop on the train and head into the city for even more options!

COSPLAY SHOWCASE
ETERNAL CON 2015

Danni Petersen
Steven Universe

Nicole Tolerico
Stargirl Bombshell

Theresa Rodrigues
Jurassic Park Ranger

Scott Lind
Jedi

Alyssa Plume
Battle Belle

Mason Byrnes & Michael Byrnes
Jimmy Olsen & Superman

Amanda Giattino
Ryuko Matoi

Shahpour Fuse
Mr. Spock

Angelina Carter
Lt. Uhura

Daniel Kazanowitz
Skull Kid

Nicholas Plume
Moon Knight

Xavier Becote Cowan
Darth Vader

Tia Cherie Polik
Red Queen

William Robbie Jr.
Cobra Commander

Evan Hillel
Black Power Ranger

Rocco Chierichella
Deadshot

Dimitrios Haritos, Chris Haritos,
Stephen Carabello, Jemal Flores
The Ghostbusters

COSPLAY SHOWCASE
ETERNAL CON 2015

Pauline Rippel
Edward Elric

Shaylyn Murphy
Ryuko Matoi

Akiim Becote
Sun Wukong

Owen Rodriguez
Mankind

Amanda Giattino
Panty

Erin D'Entremont
Snow White

Allie Eibeler
Sleeping Beauty

Dan Hoffman
Arno Dorian

Michael Flood
Green Lantern

James Murphy
Jedi

Chris Haritos
Superman

Samia Fakih
Green Arrow

Andrew Arkham Cosplay
Green Lantern

Nicole Oliva
Sailor Moon

Kurt Smith & Shannon Pilkington
Zombies

Erin D'Entremont
Scarlet Witch

Allie Eibeler
Black Widow

Naomi Goldman
Jem

Nicole Tolerico
Supergirl

Harneys Melo
Viking Stormtrooper

Giving Back Through Cosplay

Photos provided by Michael Wilson & Jason Evans

By Carrie Wood

For lots of cosplayers, their hobby is just that – a hobby, a fun way to spend their weekends a few times a year. For some, though, they've taken their cosplay passion to a different level, and have used it to give back to the community. With the mass appeal of superheroes, it's become easy for many cosplayers to use their creative talents to make appearances in-character to put a smile on a child's face.

Michael Wilson, who also is known by Knightmage online, has participated in more than 250 charity events since he began cosplaying, and actually was appearing at charity events before he attended his first convention. Once he appeared at his first party as Spider-Man and saw the young faces light up, he knew it was an opportunity to expand on.

"It reminded me of how I felt as a kid, and even now as an adult, when I see someone in costume. From that, it went into thinking of the whole cosplaying thing on a different level," he said. "I make these costumes as a creative outlet

for myself. I don't cosplay as a means for profit. So I wanted my creations to actually mean something other than something just for me."

Wilson said that he enjoys the charity work that he does because of the impact that seeing a superhero in real life can have on children.

"Putting on a costume is powerful in so many ways," he said. "It can brighten the day of a sick child, make a birthday even more special, make a parade a little more exciting, or be a show piece to help raise money."

Jason Evans, who attends charitable causes as Superman, began in 2014 after he went to some comic conventions and saw the impact that it had on kids; as a father himself, Evans enjoys that he can portray a strong character and provide a role model for kids. Evans' first hospital visit in-character left a significant mark on him.

"I've been very lucky to have three healthy kids, and I hadn't been exposed

Wilson said. "But then you really think about the situation. You start to think about how, if only for a moment, you were able to brighten that child's day. That itself is very powerful. So – you can imagine – it can be a rollercoaster ride of emotions. Still, the most important thing though is how that child is feeling, not you."

For the cosplayers who are interested in taking the first step towards participating in such charity events, Evans said it's not particularly difficult to do – and that he hopes more cosplayers are inspired to do so in the future.

"Reach out to hospitals, attend festivals, join a group, start a group, or just visit someone that you know needs a little bit of a boost," Evans said. "I know of several different groups of people that use cosplay for charitable causes, and I'm honored to be a part of them. Recently, we lost one of the most charitable people that I've ever met. Lenny Robinson – the 'Route 29 Batman' or 'Baltimore Batman' – was killed in an unfortunate accident. I'm hoping that, although we lost Lenny, the news about his death and previous charitable activities will set others into motion."

Wilson, who not only appears nearly every other week at an event in-character but also sells prints in order to raise money for charity, also offered some advice to cosplayers who want to devote a lot of time to charity. He said that the most important thing is that the charity itself is aware of who the cosplayer is and what they're doing.

"Even if your intentions are good, you don't want an organization coming back

to this type of environment before, so it hit me pretty hard. At first I had a difficult time processing what I was seeing. Seeing little kids dealing with major medical issues was difficult to comprehend," Evans said. "Being able to alleviate that for a little bit or to put a smile on their face, even momentarily, is worth any hassle that I have to deal with to make it happen."

Wilson also discussed the impact that the hospital visits can have on the cosplayers that participate.

"It's a very bittersweet feeling... you go in and see these children with medical conditions and injuries that you can't even imagine. It truly breaks your heart," Wilson said.

and claiming that they have no idea who you are. Keep a log of your receipts, and of how much you donated," he said. "Remember that when fundraising for an organization, you're also a representation of them. So always stay professional and kind."

Wilson also suggested that cosplayers have a charity and cosplay-focused résumé available for organizations that are perhaps on the fence about it.

"Get a background check done on yourself. You need to be able to instill trust with the organizations. Every hospital has their guidelines, from how the costume looks, to the person inside it," he said. "Don't be discouraged if you get denied – try and try again. Remember, the guidelines and rules are set to protect not only you, but more importantly the patients."

Both Evans and Wilson encourage the other cosplayers they know to get more involved; their charitable efforts and the efforts of many others have certainly proved that cosplay can be much more than booth babes at conventions. And, best of all, it's a rewarding experience for both the cosplayers and the kids.

"Every single event has had some memorable moments," Wilson said. "Some are silly, some are uplifting, and some really make you think and count your blessings. It's really opened my eyes further to the power of not only the fictional characters, but also those who wear the costumes. It's made me want to work harder."

Photos by Carrie Wood

AR: When I make costumes I just try to make them the best I can. For my princess costumes, I usually spare no expense and try to go the extra mile to make something no one else has or can easily replicate. I try to make the costume my own, and that includes imported trim, rhinestones, silk, et cetera. I choose a character based on who I can identify with, or something that has stuck with me for a long time.

I do make my own costumes, though when it comes to things like armor, props or metalwork, I admit I do receive help or trade to have an exchange of crafts and artistry.

What was your first introduction to the cosplay hobby? What was it about cosplay that made you want to participate?

Allen Ryde (AR): I first got into actual cosplay in 2006, though my interest in costumes started much earlier. I had made costumes for myself of Jack Skellington from *The Nightmare Before Christmas* and Grim from *The Grim Adventures of Billy and Mandy*. After attending Otakon, I realized there was so much fun to be had. It was a really positive experience and I enjoyed the fandoms and the people.

It seemed awesome to be able to go to an event in costume and have people recognize you and interact with you as a character. Disney World also helped spur the whole costuming thing with their character actors.

What is your personal approach to your costumes? How do you choose what character to emulate? Do you tend to make your own outfits, or do you receive help?

What was one of your best and most memorable experiences in cosplay?

AR: The best moments for me in cosplay are when children recognize me as a Disney character in my costumes, especially Disney princess costumes, and I can make their day and bring happiness and joy.

One time I went to the Pennsylvania Fairy Festival as Princess Aurora from *Sleeping Beauty,* and the entire day I was surrounded by small children who all wanted to see Princess Aurora. Everyone wanted hugs and pictures and would tell me how much they loved "my" movie and asked where my prince was. This also applied to some of adults who were just as excited as the children, and some of them were reacting as if they had seen a unicorn!

Cosplay is NOT Consent

By Carrie Wood

It should be obvious: if it's unwelcome behavior outside of a convention, it's probably unwelcome behavior inside the convention. And yet, over the last few years, a movement has started and gained significant momentum in the cosplay and convention community in reaction to said unwelcome behavior; the Cosplay is Not Consent movement was created in response to the rampant harassment that cosplayers often end up facing while trying to enjoy their hobby.

For whatever reason, the excuse given by many of these sort of folks when caught and confronted about their behaviors seems to always be, "Well, they're dressed like that, so they're asking for it."

Here's the problem with that reasoning: uh, no they're not.

A costume does not imply consent to anything – it never has, and it never will. And yet, there are people who can't seem to grasp this idea.

Entering a convention in costume or out of one *does* end up carrying some consent with it, however. Most conventions have in their terms of the badge of entry itself a publicity policy

that tends to state something along the lines of: "By entering this event you consent to being photographed or recorded and your image may be used in publicity materials." That, however, isn't really the issue here. Most people are going to be okay with having a fun candid photo show up online. The kind of photo that cosplayers take issue with is the one focusing on certain body parts that are clearly *not* being used for "publicity purposes."

When a cosplayer puts on a costume and heads through the doors of a convention, they're not simultaneously putting on a sign that reads "Please come over and touch me without asking first." People don't just randomly go up to a stranger on the streets and give them an unsolicited hug. People don't go up to someone they don't know and straight-up tackle them from behind. And yet, these are the kind of incidents that have persisted at conventions over the years. I've spent some time with cosplayers who have had a wide variety of experiences regarding this topic at conventions over the years, and I hope that by adding their insight to my own, a clearer picture of the problem and the solutions can be found.

Sexual Harassment

One of the biggest issues regarding sexual harassment is that every individual has a different definition of it, and every individual responds to it differently. Generally, "sexual harassment" is defined as any sort of bullying or coercion of a sexual nature. However, while one person may consider an action harassment, another may consider it playful flirting. Basically, if someone is being made to feel uncomfortable based on the way they look or the way they are dressed, chances are that person would say they feel sexually harassed.

Because of how many popular characters – in comics, video games, anime, and more – are designed, cosplayers often end up showing more skin in a convention than they would on a regular basis. That's not to say that only those who are dressed more skimpy than usual are the only ones facing harassment at conventions; plenty of fully-clothed folks end up dealing with the same awful behavior from their fellow congoers. The entire convention atmosphere lends itself to seeing a lot of this kind of behavior, simply because it's not "out in public," and that ends up causing problems.

As someone who's been cosplaying since 2003, I've dealt with harassers a few times over the years. One costume in particular got me more attention than I bargained for – a red bunny suit from the series *Higurashi: When They Cry*. I got a lot of looks, but given that my everything was everywhere, I kind of expected looks. (I don't think anyone who dresses in a "sexy" outfit at a convention *doesn't* expect looks.) What I didn't expect was the amount of people who would try and sneak photographs of just my behind. I didn't expect the people who asked me to "come hang out" in their hotel room with them. I didn't expect to be literally followed around the convention by a group of men who didn't know how to take "no" for an answer.

I've never had a problem telling people off, so most of these creepers got an earful. And given that I always travel in a small group around conventions, I felt uncomfortable but never unsafe. But, every person reacts differently to this sort of behavior. Delaware cosplayer Jerry Farmer recounted an incident from a convention in 2009 that he witnessed.

"I was waiting outside the green room for the masquerade cosplay competition when we heard a girl yelling at a guy. She was dressed as Yoko from *Gurren Lagann* – a bikini top with some short shorts and combat boots – and from what we heard of the argument, this guy had been following her around for a while," he said. "Because what we caught was something along the lines of, 'You've been bothering me all day! Get the hell away from me!' He protested, and she kicked him in the pills."

Another cosplayer who was on the receiving end of some unwanted attention was Vikki Hughes. She said that as she mostly cosplays as male characters, she hasn't experienced too many unwanted advances or insults – since it seems most of those are directed towards people who are dressed as female characters. However, at one particular convention she was dressed as Sailor Star Healer from *Sailor Moon*, which is basically a bra with booty shorts and thigh-high boots, making it her most exposing costume to date.

"While in it, my friend dressed as Sailor Moon had a guy come up and ask for a hug. My friend politely refused, and the man protested – 'Come on, it's just a hug!' I stood up and yelled at him to back off, and he did, looking startled," Hughes said. "At least he asked, I guess? Later in the same costume, I was working at a booth in the dealer's room selling merchandise. Guys would ask for a picture with me and try to put their arm around me frequently – never a problem when I was dressed as a male character. It was very uncomfortable."

These stories are unfortunately not uncommon in the cosplay scene. It seems as though every cosplayer who has ever dared to show off a little skin has dealt with sexual harassment from other congoers. But the Cosplay is Not Consent movement encompasses more than that.

Other Unwanted Touching

The idea of consent should apply to just about any interaction with a cosplayer at a convention. Yet, there are cosplayers who have dealt with people taking their photo without asking first, or, worse, being outright tackled by another congoer. This is just yet another instance of social norms being tossed into the garbage by convention attendees – there are people who truly believe that simply because they are at a convention, acting like a complete loon is acceptable.

"I have frequently had total strangers leap onto me, into my arms or onto my back while I'm in cosplay, either 'in character' or because they are such big fans of the character I'm dressed as," Hughes said. "I have had props broken by this behavior."

Another cosplayer, Mike Pfeffer from New Jersey, elaborated on the idea that sneaking up and tackling someone is never okay, based on his experience at Otakon in Baltimore, MD.

"I've always been really, *really* bad at getting snuck up on. I hate it, it kind of gets me hyperventilating. It's not a good feeling – I scare very easily. I'm going across the skywalk from the Baltimore Convention Center to the Inner Harbor to get some lunch. Then, suddenly, I get hurled off to the right," he said. "Some girl who I didn't know had executed a jumping hug onto my left side. On my right was my giant prop that was kind of fragile, being

Cosplayer Vikki Hughes
Photo by gryfeathr Photography

made out of foam core and thick dowels, but the second she did that – at a serious running force – I thought I was going to die, then and there. She shouted and grinned at me, then ran into the Inner Harbor area.

"I was holding myself up on the banister of the skywalk, just holding my chest. It seriously felt like I was going to have a heart attack then and there, or that I could have been pushed over the skywalk onto the busy street below," Pfeffer continued. "It's nowhere near the consent that cosplayers face from sexual harassment creepers, being expected to somehow be okay with being treated awfully, I know that. But jumping onto someone without their consent is so totally not okay. It doesn't matter if you're a six-foot dude or a five-foot girl. It was a really awful experience and I still remember it today."

What can be done about it?

Despite what some people might tell you, the solution is *not* "If people didn't dress like that we wouldn't have these problems." Cosplayers absolutely have the right to dress as whatever character they choose in whatever way they choose without having to fear some guy grabbing their butt or a flying tackle coming out of nowhere. Just because

Cosplayer Vikki Hughes - Photo by Kacie Doran

someone is dressed in a costume or as a specific character does not make them any human or any less deserving of respect and decency.

Thankfully, the conventions themselves have started taking charge on their own, forming strict anti-harassment policies (that are often accompanied with large signs that read "Cosplay is Not Consent" on the show floor). New York Comic Con is one of these conventions, with a pretty comprehensive list of what harassing behaviors are.

According to NYCC's Harassment Policy, the convention takes a zero tolerance approach to behaviors including but not limited to: "stalking, offensive verbal comments, harassing or non-consensual photography or recording, bathroom policing, unwelcome physical attention, intimidation, physical assault and/or battery, sustained disruption of panels, signings, and other events, and inappropriate physical contact." This is in relation to factors such as race, gender identity, sexual orientation, body size, appearance, age, gender, gender presentation, among many other things. Those who are reported as being in violation of this policy can get kicked out of the convention with no refund.

This is exactly the kind of policy that needs to be in place at every convention. Despite all of the best wishes and hopes in the world that people will behave themselves while at a convention, the fact that the Cosplay is Not Consent movement even exists proves otherwise.

So, cosplayers: what should you do when you're being harassed? If nothing else, **report it!** Grab your nearest convention staff or security person and point out the person who's been causing you problems. Not everyone is comfortable with confronting someone who's harassing them, and that's fine; we're not going to advocate for that, because that's not a good approach for every situation. However, the people who can truly do something about it (the convention staff) need to be informed so that the person being a creep or harasser is either given the opportunity to recognize their bad behavior and change it, or be removed from the event entirely.

And if you're accused of harassing someone? First off, apologize! Everyone should be able to feel comfortable at a convention, and if you did something to make someone else uncomfortable, apologize for it and make sure it doesn't happen again. It's also entirely possible that a miscommunication happened, if Jerry Farmer's story proves anything.

"As I came into the convention center, I spotted a cosplayer in an absolutely gorgeous dress. I wanted a picture, so I asked. Except that my sentences got crossed, I was talking too fast, and what should have been 'That's a really pretty dress, can I take your picture please?' instead came out as 'Can I take your dress, please?' Oops," he said. "I caught myself and apologized right away, and I asked again properly, because that could have gone in so many ways. Anyone can come across as a creeper, but as long as you realize that this can be, and as long as people are sane and understanding, a lot of problems can be avoided or resolved."

The most important thing to do is *ask* – get consent! Do you want a photo of someone? Ask first. Do you want to take your photo with your arm around them? Ask first. Do you want a hug from someone dressed as your favorite character? Ask first. Don't invade someone's personal space without their consent, and these problems will eventually, hopefully, disappear entirely.

Cosplayer Diary: The Cosplay Generation Gap

By Eddie Newsome

Photo: Kacie Doran

Like all hobbies, cosplay has seen a slow and steady evolution over the years. What was once relegated to small sewing rooms has changed into large workshops; what was previously worked on only with a thread and needle now sees creative usage of Worbla, craft foam, and even fiberglass.

Though there's been an obvious shift in materials and setting, there's been a less noticeable change in how cosplay is addressed and accepted. If you look at how compact and secluded the cosplay world was 15 or 20 years ago, and compare it to now, you will see a huge shift regarding creativity and ingenuity. That shift has taken place slowly over time.

If you look closely, you'll also see a noticeable difference in age groups. When I first started, cosplay was about paying homage to heroes – or even villains – that inspired you, or that you identified with. Now, it seems more people say that they cosplay because of how trendy a character is, or what the newest design or concept happens to be. I don't fault anyone for this, but it's just another example of changing times.

Does a generational gap exist? Yes, it does – and it can be seen at any convention or on any cosplay website. I've seen more of the younger cosplayers go over the top in terms of being in character, or even how they carry themselves. Is this a bad thing? Well, it depends on your point of view. While I have a "live and let live" attitude, I feel as though sometimes things get out of hand as far as "staying in character." I've seen teenaged cosplayers run around screaming – "in character" – and then get upset when they get odd looks from other attendees. At past conventions I've done what I can to make sure that cosplayers don't outright act like jerks, reminding them that these things are fine, but in moderation.

Obviously, not everyone has run into these issues, and not every convention ends up with cosplayers acting out of line. And of course, not every cosplayer from my generation is stern and serious all the time, either. With time and age also comes experience, as well as an enlightened insight in how we carry ourselves at conventions and look at the social situations that arise at cons. As they say, ignorance truly is bliss, but with that ignorance comes some relatively simple misunderstandings. So, my question to the older generation is – do we take it upon ourselves to show younger cosplayers how things worked "back in our day," or do we let them figure it out on their own and just hope for the best? Something to think about!

Cosplayer Spotlight: Damaris Degen

Please introduce yourself!
Damaris Degen (DD): My name is Damaris Degen, and I'm a mother to two amazing twin boys, Ethan and Justin Degen.

Do you tend to make your costumes yourself? What are your strengths in regards to costume construction?
DD: Yes, I try to make my own, but usually call upon the help of my friends that also are a part of this ever growing community. My biggest strengths are creativity and craftsmanship. I sculpt, draw, mold and cast. I'm also a professional graphic designer so I have a lot of artistic skills. I also love to bring in the "wow" factor. I love to stay fit and be true to the character.

What's been one of your best or most memorable experiences with cosplay?
DD: While volunteering for Toys for Tots with Costumers with a Cause, the most

Photos provided by Damaris Degen

memorable moment for me was when this little girl ran up to me and hugged my leg yelling, "Spider-Woman, Spider-Woman!" It melted my heart!

Another time was when I volunteered for the Children's Cancer Center at Arnold Palmer Hospital. That was very emotional for me since my son, Ethan, was undergoing chemotherapy treatment for his Optic Glioma due to his genetic illness of NF-1. It reminded me how fortunate I am, and to value and appreciate the time I have with my son because no matter what, things could have been far worse. I count my blessings every day.

What challenges or issues do you think cosplayers face the most?
DD: To be a cosplayer is to be a fan. It's not just about putting on a costume, doing a photoshoot then having a fancy gallery. The world will critique your craft, work or size. Bullies come in all forms and they are definitely within the cosplay community. Just remember, you are costuming for yourself, no one else. You don't need any approval other than your own.

What do you think cosplay adds to the overall convention experience?
DD: I believe that cosplaying has added another level to the convention-going experience. It's fun to see someone dressed up as your favorite character and see how much work they put into their craft.

Any final thoughts you'd like to share?
DD: You know that little voice inside you? It's your inner child that wants to come out and show the world that you're passionate about your fandom. Let them out!

RACE AND COSPLAY

By Carrie Wood

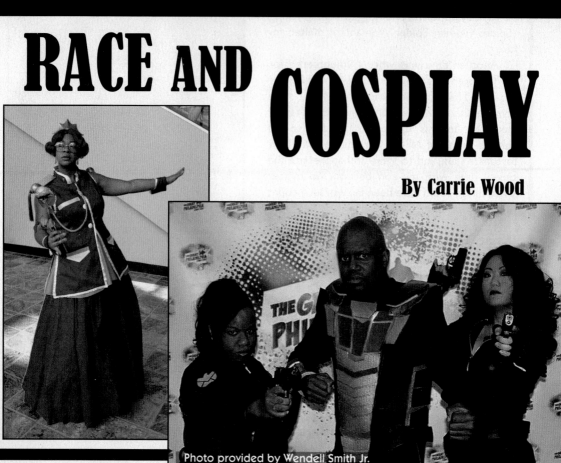

Photo by Carrie Wood

Photo provided by Wendell Smith Jr.

The nerd community at large has always been diverse. There's nothing precluding anyone of any demographic from taking in the joys that comic books, video games, cartoons, television and film provide. So the cosplay community, as a subset of "nerd culture," sees much of the same sort of diversity. There's nothing stopping someone with an Asian background from cosplaying Batman, or someone with an African background from cosplaying Black Widow – regardless of ethnicity, there shouldn't be any barriers preventing people from cosplaying specific characters.

And yet, there has been an unfortunate trend within the realm of cosplay that seems to want to put up walls that restrict access to certain characters; comments online can be seen all over the place, with remarks such as "You're too dark for Wonder Woman" ranging all the way to straight-up racist slurs.

Cosplayer Tiffany Witcher, who is African-American, said that she's faced the worst sort of harassment for cosplaying "outside her race."

"[People would tell me] that I can't cosplay a character because it's 'not in your skin color,'" she said. "I've been called things like monkey, coon, and even the N-word... There's multiple issues in the community right now, which really pushes black cosplayers back a little, and stops people from doing it in the future, too."

Often, non-white cosplayers are told by others to only cosplay characters that match their race, which can leave a bad taste in the mouths of many.

"When I first started cosplaying, I did get a lot of people who tried to convince me to sort of 'stay within my race,'" Alex Li, better known as Allen Ryde, said. "Even now, there are people who still believe that you're somehow limited – or should be limited – to cosplaying certain characters. Which is ridiculous."

Photo by Carrie Wood

Photo provided by Tiffany Witcher

Ryde is a Chinese-American cosplayer from the Baltimore area who not only cosplays characters that are traditionally seen as a different race, but also a different gender. He cosplays Disney princesses as often as he cosplays princes, and despite having an immense and palpable love for the source material, has dealt with a swath of criticism regarding his characters of choice over the years.

"People continue to tell me that because of my race, or my gender, that I'll never be 'accurate' enough, or that it's somehow some sort of mistake or travesty that I'm continuing to cosplay certain characters," he said. "And that can be really damaging. I put effort and time into my costumes. I like to sort of get back at these kinds of people by taking my costumes and entering them into contests and taking home Best in Show or Best Craftsmanship."

While Ryde immediately jumped into cosplay via characters of other ethnic back-grounds, some other cosplayers instead choose characters that they feel are a "better match" to begin with. Wendell Smith, Sr. said that the race of the characters influenced his decision to cosplay them – at first.

"When I first started cosplaying, I went for characters who represent me, meaning African or African-American – Black Panther, John Stewart, Mace Windu, and so on," he said. "After a while, I decided to do characters that fit my personality a little better. I've done Thanos, Darkseid, Colossus, and even a gender-bent Kitty Pryde. My change in choice was based more on an increased familiarity with cosplay, and making more friends who are cosplayers."

Smith said that he believes the race issue has persisted in the cosplay community because of "one simple word – ignorance."

"There are people who will troll anything they don't fully understand, or cannot do themselves," he said. "In the six years I've been cosplaying, I haven't seen or heard

Photos provided by Tiffany Witcher

Photo provided by Wendell Smith Jr.

anything negative towards myself. However, I have seen hateful things said about friends and acquaintances. 'Oh, she is the Black version of this,' 'Oh, he's too dark to represent that character,' or 'I didn't know they made such-and-such for Black people.'"

The biggest source of controversy within the cosplay community in regards to race has seemed to revolve around a cosplayer choosing to use makeup to look like someone of a difference race – both when someone wants to make themselves look paler, or when someone wants to make themselves look darker. There's a pretty clear divide on this. Many say that trying to appear as a different ethnicity is racist 100 percent of the time, while others say that it's a more nuanced situation.

"I personally feel that a person does not need to change their skin color to represent a person of another color," Smith said. "However, if someone takes the time to tastefully change their skin color, and not

make a mockery of the person, or race of that person, it's a different story."

Ryde agreed, and elaborated on his own experience with cosplay makeup in the business of being a party princess, where a certain look is often expected by clients.

"I don't have much room to critique on that front, because I myself have used makeup to make myself look more like a different race, and even a different gender, than what I am," he said. "In the world of princessing, where we're doing long gigs, sometimes six to eight hours, my makeup is pretty heavy and I do use a bit of a lighter color to give that impression. That's just how the game works."

Ryde also discussed the issue that seems to arise more when a lighter-skinned person tries to make themselves look darker, as opposed to the reverse.

"I feel like if people of color can use makeup to make themselves look fairer or of a different ethnicity, I don't necessarily

Photo by Carrie Wood

Beauty and the Beast. The Broadway version of that show has debuted in countries all over the world, so she's been portrayed as having different ethnicities. She's been African, she's been Spanish, she's been Japanese – and so on. It's a very flexible thing," he said. "Sometimes the shows even alter her costume a little bit to better reflect her background in that version of the show, too. So if they can do that in an official production, then there's nothing stopping anyone from cosplaying any character regardless of what their ethnicity is."

Smith, meanwhile, has been working to spread more of an awareness of the race issue in cosplay via social media campaigns.

"To counter [the racism] and educate people about cosplayers of other cultures, a few of us started a campaign in February called '28 Days of Black Cosplay.' We received a lot of positive feedback," he said. "And then there was some negative feedback, from both white and Black cosplayers. It was an interesting campaign. I can't wait to do it all over again – with the good and the bad that came from it all."

So, the big question – what can be done about the racism that persists in the cosplay community?

"Brutal answer? People need to get their heads out of their butts," Smith said. "A more PC answer is that people need to step back and realize that people can cosplay any character of their choice, regardless of color, race, creed, size, sex, and so on. Cosplay is for fun! There is *no room* for racists, bigots, body-shaming, or sexists."

Witcher offered advice that can not only be applied to the continuing race issue in the cosplay world, but to the hobby as a whole.

"Spread positivity, as much as you can to the community. If you do something to brighten up someone's day where they've been put down, then they might go on to spread it further," she said. "For me, I try to help against bullies in the community and outside it. If I can help just a little, it could always spread and go a long way for people. It takes so much more energy to be negative to someone than to be positive."

see how it's so much more shameful when the reverse happens," Ryde said. "And that still falls into the whole thing where it needs to be done tastefully and to the best of their ability."

Witcher emphasized the point that despite someone's best intentions, they could always offend someone else with regards to race-bending makeup.

"This is a difficult subject for me every time," she said. "I feel that making yourself a race that doesn't exist is fine, but on the other side, [making yourself a different race that does exist] has so much history with it that it can offend people. I have no issue with tanning – none at all – but I always say to be careful not to do makeup that could possibly offend someone."

What's important to keep in mind for cosplayers who are a different race than who they are dressing as, says Ryde, is that there really is hardly ever a set standard for that character's background.

"There are a lot of cases where a certain character has been portrayed in multiple ethnicities. For example, take Belle from

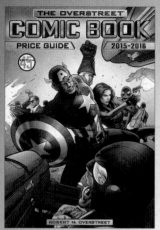

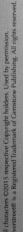
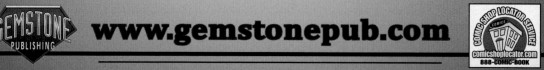

Cosplayer Diary: Race in Cosplay

By Eddie Newsome

When I wake up on the day of a convention, a photoshoot or an appearance, and I look in the mirror, who do I see? Do I see an African-American cosplayer? Do I just see a cosplayer? Or do I see a man who is cosplaying someone of a different race? The correct answer is all three – race always has and always will be one of the prominent subjects in cosplay, and in a non-post-racial society it will continue to be. I have had the honor – and the dismay – of seeing both sides to this subject first-hand.

Let's flash back about five years. I had just read *Truth: Red, White & Black* by Kyle Baker and Robert Morales. This book spoke to me in such a way that I had to bring the character of Isaiah Bradley to life. As a cosplayer I consider myself blessed if just once in my life a character speaks to the essence of who I am at my core – and this book did just that. I arrived at San Diego Comic Con with pride in what I was doing in cosplaying Isaiah Bradley. I even met Kyle Baker, his creator, and Baker's expression showed nothing but approval in my execution of it.

But when I was shown on the Marvel Comics website in my costume, I was bombarded with negative comments, including people calling me "Captain N-Word" and so on. Thankfully, in the midst of this, people started coming to my defense with historical content of who I was cosplaying. There was no room for hate with such a positive thing like cosplaying the Black Captain America.

On the flip side of things, I saw a white woman decide that she wanted to cosplay Michonne from *The Walking Dead*, which is great – but she did it in blackface, which began an uproar on social media of pure backlash. Her reasoning was that she wanted to be true to the character. The problem here was putting on that kind of makeup either without knowing or choosing to ignore the history behind that action, so the execution of the character was done in pretty poor taste. The excuse was given of "why doesn't anyone get upset when someone paints their face red to be an alien," and that's a sorry one; the truth is, aliens don't exist, and there isn't a negative history behind a fictional creature as there is with the history of blackface.

Now, let's look at a different female cosplayer, who wanted to cosplay Storm from the X-Men franchise. She had the tiara, contacts, and the hair to the exact specifications of the character in the book, and the internet loved it – and she was white! I bring this up to make a point – that it's possible for people to cosplay a character of a different race without undermining someone else's race or ethnic background.

This, I feel, is the root of the race in cosplay dilemma: when we totally associate cosplay as race-specific, we all lose as a community. Yes, we need more people of color (and by color I mean more than just African-American) in comics, anime and in movies. But until that day arrives, why not embrace the diversity that we have in our community, without disrespecting anyone or cosplaying from the source material in a way that can be seen as negative? How many times have you seen or heard on a blog or website, "oh, that's a great Asian Superman," or "You're pretty for a black Wonder Woman?" As I step back and view the cosplay world, I have begun to notice a trend that with these cosplay faux pas, the majority of the time they're made by people who don't care or don't know about the history; when the history of a race or ethnicity or even history of cosplay itself is overlooked, we see these problems of race rear their ugly head. When this problem arrives, is it always about racial sensitivity? Not by a long shot – sometimes it's a simple misunderstanding.

What's needed now is an open, honest dialogue about race in cosplay, and how we can honor characters without offending anyone. Hopefully this can be the first salvo in what is an ongoing challenge regarding the understanding and respect that is often lacking in cosplay.

COSPLAY AS A CAREER

BY CARRIE WOOD

For most, cosplay is a hobby. It's a fun and creative outlet to express their love of a series, meet other people who enjoy the same things that they do, and experience their fandom. But for some others, cosplay is more than just an occasional thing – it's become a job. We spoke with cosplayers about how they've been able to take their hobby and turn it into a money-making enterprise for them.

The Prop Maker

Like many cosplayers, Jason Osborne didn't get into the hobby with the goal of making things for others. But once he honed his own talent, especially in regards to props, he began assisting friends and now has a full online store full of custom-made replicas from popular shows and video games. Osborne, who also goes by the moniker of CeruleanDraco online, said that his business grew simply out of doing work for friends, and then having word of mouth get around that his work was worth it. He's been making props now for the last few years.

"I have been making props for a long time and am constantly learning new things and improving my skills, but I have been confident in my work to sell them for the last three years or so," he said. "Although I do look back on certain items I have made and want to remake them, because I have improved so much."

Osborne has been able to use his prop production as a moneymaking venture that supplements his regular income thanks to the flexibility of his job,

"Until recently, prop-making was my primary source, but a job opportunity presented itself very near to where I live, so it has become more of a 50-50 thing," he said. "My job is contract-based, so I work for a few weeks at a time while still making props at a slower pace. Then, when my contract is up, it's full force again until I get called with another opportunity."

He described his greatest success so far in regards to his props as the now-iconic Scissor Blade from the anime series *Kill La Kill*. Osborne said he's now made dozens of them and is still not bored of making them. However, his favorite piece in his portfolio is the Lance of Longinus from *Neon Genesis Evangelion*.

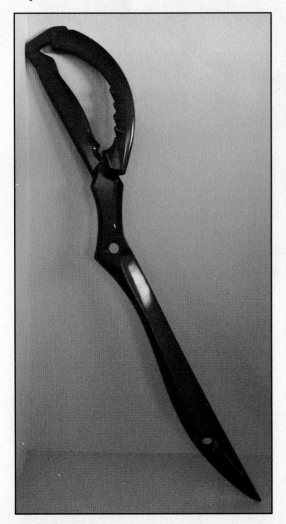

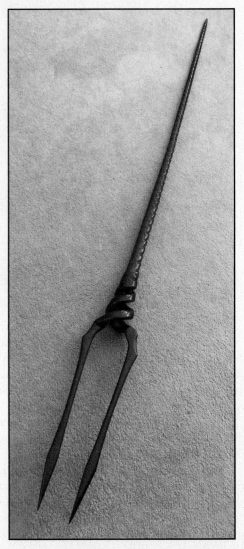

"I posted a list of my 'dream props' and a friend of mine saw that I wanted to make the lance," he said. "We talked about it and after six months of on-and-off work and some failed attempts, it finally came out *exactly* as I wanted!"

Though he hasn't had any roadblocks in his ventures, Osborne did mention the time requirement for prop commissions.

"I do wish curing and drying times for resin, paints, and other materials didn't exist. I get focused on making things and it's hard to have to drop something for the rest of the day because your resin needs 16 hours to cure," he said.

For those looking to get into cosplay as a business, Osborne advised one key thing: "Do something that you love."

"For me, it was scissor blades and other props from anime and games that I was already a fan of, so it was always fun," he said. "It can be really hard to motivate yourself to work on something you don't care for. Also, stay positive and diligent!"

The Clothier

Jerry Farmer had already been crafting for himself for a number of years before he

took his first commission. The Delaware native said that while he never made a conscious decision to start making costumes for others, after taking on projects for some friends in 2012, things "just sort of took off from there." Farmer eventually came to the realization that he enjoyed what he was doing so much that he could do it as a job.

"I think it was the combination of having a number of people start asking me for outfits, and realizing that I enjoyed the

sewing – even on a deadline, and even with the headaches involved in doing costumes for others – more than I enjoyed the temp work I was pulling at the time," he said. "It just kept growing and growing as more and more people were satisfied with my work for them, and told their friends, or came back for seconds, thirds, fourths… fifths. I think I realized I'd essentially started my own business when someone asked me how many commissions I'd done that year and I could not remember."

Farmer said that while there are plenty of benefits to the job – such a setting your own hours, getting to do something you enjoy, and seeing yourself improve at your craft very quickly – there are definitely some pitfalls.

"If you want to succeed at this – if you want to turn it into a source of income that is going to keep a roof over your head, gas in the car, food on the table, and the lights on – it has to be a full-time job," he said.

In fact, it probably has to be *more* than full-time.

"Once you decide that it's going to be your primary source of income, you are basically saying, 'I will work 50-plus hours a week at this.' You don't get Saturdays or Sundays off," Farmer said.

Farmer offered some advice for those looking to turn their costume-making hobby into a full-time gig, saying that communication and organization a big part of what need to happen in order to be successful at it.

"Talk it out with your partner or spouse and with your roommates. They need to understand that what you are doing is becoming a full-time, bill-paying job. Set expectations so that they understand that you are working. Otherwise, it becomes very easy for them see you as unemployed," he said. "Also, keep records. If you're good, you're going to get repeat customers, and it helps to know costs, measurements, and what you're going to need to charge. Keeping track of your hours and expenses is necessary, too; that way you know if you're under-charging. It also makes doing your taxes easier!"

Other ideas for those getting started include setting up your own workspace – one that is yours, and nobody else's – that is secluded and allows you to get your work done efficiently; also, be sure to draft a contract form and a generic order form to set terms and conditions on the project. However, Farmer said that the most important thing that full-time costume-makers need to do is be willing to push through the hard parts to see a project to the end.

"You have to put in the necessary time, and you have to keep improving at your work. This is not a field for those who are not self-starters, nor for those who allow themselves to get distracted. Some of the world will be dull and tedious," Farmer said. "You'll be making your 50th petticoat, or you'll be doing the same blasted invisible zipper for the 100th time, and you will like it, and you will keep at it, or you will fail."

Cosplayer Spotlight:
Oliviazira

Please introduce yourself!

Olivazira: Hi! I'm Olivia or Azira, or Oliviazira, basically whatever you want to call me. I also answer to 'Hey you!' I'm from Boston, and I recently graduated from fashion design school.

What was your first introduction to the cosplay hobby? What was it about cosplay that made you want to participate?

Olivazira: My first introduction to cosplay was seeing pictures of cosplayers online when I was in the fifth grade or so. I thought the people in the pictures looked so cool that I wanted to try it myself. My first cosplay I wore to anime con was when I was probably 12.

What is your personal approach to your costumes? How do you choose what character to emulate? Do you tend to make your own outfits, or do you receive help?

Olivazira: Personally, I mix 'Would I look good as this character?' with 'I'm going to do whatever the hell I feel like,' with mixed results. I won't cosplay from a series I've never watched or read myself, or a character I absolutely hate. (Though I made that mistake once. Pro-tip, never decide who you are going to be from watching only the opening credits of the

first episode.) Generally, I choose characters I really like from series I love. I make everything myself for the most part. I sometimes get help with things like wig styling since I am absolutely useless when it comes to that.

How has the community changed over the years?

Olivazira: I think the cosplay community has changed a lot in a short time. Gone are the times of 'This wig color does not exist in real life' and 'I have no idea how anyone would do this.' Now people face 'I hope I'm good enough' and 'I hope I am not endlessly harassed for various reasons.'

Cosplayer Spotlight: Janel McClain

What was it about cosplay that made you want to participate?
Janel McClain (JM): A large part of why I wanted to start making costumes was that sewing reminds me of my grandmother, whom I lost shortly before I started cosplaying. My grandma taught me how to sew when I was in elementary school. Of course, I didn't want to do it at the time, but I did love to have something I could wear to school or around the house that I made with my own hands. After she passed I started to sew again and it made me feel close to her, and everything grew from there.

What's been one of your best or most memorable experiences with cosplay?
JM: My most memorable cosplay moment was meeting George Pérez for the first time during my second Dragon Con. I was wearing my first sewn costume ever and as I stood there freaking out over him being there he complimented me on my Eartha Kitt 1966 Catwoman costume.

Dapper Moose photography

Photo by Brass Ivy Designs

What about one of your worst?

JM: My worst cosplay experience was when I made one of my first costumes. I made really bad material choices that left me scarred and in pain for quite some time. I found myself in the Atlanta heat stripping off parts of my armor to stop it from cutting into my skin.

What challenges or issues do you think cosplayers face the most?

JM: I think cosplayers are misunderstood and almost treated as a sideshow when local news reports on a convention. Oftentimes people outside of the community don't realize how much time, hard work, and money goes into the hobby.

What do you think cosplay adds to the overall convention experience?

JM: Cosplay brings color and vibrancy to a convention. I also feel that cosplay makes the convention a more interactive experience, because fans get to get up close with some of their favorite characters.

Any final thoughts you'd like to share?

JM: If anyone is interested in getting into cosplay I think they should just go for it. There are so many sources online to help you along, and once you're in you'll be hooked.

Photo by
Bryan Humphrey/
Mad Scientist
with a camera

Photo by
Andrew Haworth

Photo by Mike Kowalek / Eleventh photograph

Cosplay from the Creator's Perspective

By J.C. Vaughn

Rob Liefeld was tired and he looked it.

The former *wunderkind* and *enfant terrible* of Marvel Comics and onetime spokesperson for Levi's buttonfly 501 jeans, one of the original founders of Image Comics, had just worked a line of eager fans like he was the one who invented the process. The line was, by conservative estimates, six and a half hours long.

The fans who exited the line after getting the artist's signature on their copies of *New Mutants* #98 or *Youngblood* #1

uniformly praised Liefeld's enthusiasm, and his ability to make the current fan standing in front of him feel like he or she was the first one he'd talked to all day. To a person they all said he was even better with the kids.

So when he finally finished with the line, it was entirely reasonable that he was a bit on the spent side. But then he saw the Deadpools.

The convention center had been overrun with cosplayers, and several dozen of them were variations on

Liefeld's *New Mutants* character, "the Merc with a mouth," Deadpool.

And they wanted to get a picture with The Man.

Liefeld perked right up, a new level of energy surged through a smile no one could fake. He called his son, Chase, into the picture, and urged the Deadpools to draw closer and get into character. They enthusiastically gathered around and obliged.

A creator and his children. His many, many, disturbed children.

It was a moment of comic con magic.

While fellow cosplayers and many convention attendees relish the cosplayers' efforts, perhaps no one enjoys it more than the people who created the characters in the first place. Although most of the Golden Age and many of the Silver Age greats are gone, many creators have come face-to-face with their creations.

"It's really one of the greatest experiences I've had as a creator. Finding people who love your character enough to accurately portray her, to get the details of the costume and the make-up just right, it's incredible," said writer-artist Billy Tucci. In recent years he's been more known for his award-winning tour of duty with DC's Sgt. Rock, but Tucci made his name with his creator-owned title *Shi*. The title character, an Asian-American young woman, is as deadly as she is beautiful, and she's inspired many cosplayers over the years.

"It's hard to describe what it feels like that people relate so powerfully to a character I created. It's pretty humbling," he said.

And of course it's not even just the originators of properties that get to experience this. Sometimes it's the current creative team.

While Paul Dini and Bruce Timm created Harley Quinn, current writers Amanda Conner and Jimmy Palmiotti see dozens of Harleys at virtually every convention they attend, and Palmiotti's quick to post images of them to social media.

He embraced the enthusiasm of it years ago, including using fans cosplaying his own creations on a photo cover for his Image Comics series *Creator Owned Heroes*. Palmiotti echoed Tucci's comments about how much the enthusiasm means to him as a creator.

Billy Tucci

Just before this book went to press, Marvel Comics began issuing a line of cosplay variants. While very few of the actual creators of the characters were involved, it's not unreasonable to think they would have enjoyed the experience. And that seems to go whether it's the most independent of the independents or the most mainstream of the mainstream.

And it's a two-way street.

Special effects artist Brody Williams turned cosplayers Bryan Treakle and Amber Love into Silas and Annie Belle Irons, respectively, from writer James Kuhoric's acclaimed Dynamite Entertainment mini-series *Dead Irons*.

Kuhoric, the veteran *Army of Darkness*, *Battlestar Galactica* and *Legendary Talespinners* writer, who also wrote Dynamite's *Six Million Dollar Man Season Six*, was there to see his characters come to life for a photo shoot for a cover for the upcoming *Dead Irons* sequel originally planned for 2014 (but pushed back due to his duties as Vice-President of Publishing for Avatar).

"I can't think of a more rewarding situation as a creator than to see your characters made real. The cosplay community is one of the most dedicated groups of fans in all of comics. And to have life breathed into your characters

by fans that are moved enough by your creations to make their own homemade costumes is truly humbling," Kuhoric said.

"Brody Williams' work was phenomenal," he said of the artist who turned cosplayers Bryan Treakle and Amber Love into Silas and Annie Belle Irons, respectively.

"We are talking about a young man that has more talent than many theatrical special effect houses. Over the course of the weeks leading up to the event, Brody talked with me often to get a deeper understanding of the characters in *Dead Irons*. He asked everything about the characters - their history, motivations, mannerisms, and physical description. As he developed his techniques to accomplish the makeups, he did test shots, gathered costuming, and fabricated props to be used during the photo shoot. When Brody presented the finished effects, I was staring at Silas and Annie Belle brought to life," he said.

Tiffany N. Perry as Abby from Kuhoric's *Legendary Talespinners.*

COSPLAY PHOTOGRAPHY

By Carrie Wood

Cosplayers are seen more often than ever before, and a big reason for that has to do with the rise of cosplay photography. And we're not just talking about people who wander the convention halls, snapping photos of cosplayers in the hallways to post on social media (not that there's anything wrong with that!); we're focusing a little more on the people who spend time with cosplayers at cons and outside of them, adjusting all the little folds of fabric, flipping capes to catch the wind, and so on. Cosplay photographers often put in as much work to make cosplayers look good as they do themselves, but it seems that this hobby-within-the-hobby doesn't get as much attention as it deserves.

What got many cosplay photographers interested was that they noticed how much they, as cosplayers, appreciated having a nice photo of themselves in their costumes.

"The more time I spent cosplaying, the more I realized how much good photography did for a cosplay's presentation. Pictures that were in the right environment, or taken at an interesting angle, or recreated a canon event grabbed me," cosplayer and photographer Vikki Hughes said. "I decided I wanted to become a cosplay photographer as a solid hobby when I took some photos for a friend's cosplay group and had a lot of fun arranging people and finding interesting angles to photograph from while using her very nice DSLR. Realizing that with the right equipment and practice I could create the photography I always admired inspired me."

Lauren McFadden, also a photographer who began as a cosplayer, learned that she had a love for the hobby after realizing it could help recreate scenes from her favorite media.

"The biggest factor into pursuing cosplay photography was actually wanting to provide photographer friends of mine with artsy, narrative pictures of their own cosplays, in order to thank them for always giving me beautiful photos in return," she said. "After a while, I found that I was really interested in showing people's costumes in a way that looked like they could be 'movie stills' or hyper-realistic fan art of their favorite series, and I try to hold onto that philosophy even today."

For Kacie Doran, her foray into the cosplay scene came after a couple of years seeing the world through a viewfinder.

"I had my camera for about two years before I even got into cosplay," she said. "I wanted to document things in the way that I saw them. I think everyone sees the world differently, we choose what we want to see and what we don't, and there's a million angles that you could look at something from. I just wanted to tell what I saw in those things."

DC-area photographer Archie Brown had his views of cosplay and photography mesh together naturally thanks to a photography course he happened to be taking around the time of his first anime convention.

"I had an interest in photography first, during my senior year of film school – so, 2012," he said. "I took a single-semester low credit hours course in still photography, and since I was going to my first anime con during the course, I figured on taking photos of the cosplayers there as basis for my final assignment."

McFadden said that the different approach to cosplay photography – where there's more of a focus on recreating images and atmospheres from other forms of media – allows for it to be a little more "artsy and experimental" than other forms of photography.

"You certainly don't see wedding photographers messing around with Instagram-like filters on someone's special day, but in the occasionally fantastical settings of series from which people like to cosplay, maybe that crazy color scheme is the perfect touch," she said. "That all being said, I think you end up learning a lot of skills that apply to both as well: what angles look good on people, how to light something to set the mood correctly, and gener-

Photo credit: Vikki Hughes   Cosplayer: Bur Loire

Photo credit: Lauren McFadden Cosplayer: ShinjaNinja

al fine art composition."

It's sometimes assumed that cosplay photography would be similar to any other form of portrait photography, but that's missing the mark, according to Brown.

"Portraits, at their purest, simplest level, form a personal message about the subject and who they are inside, turning them 'inside out,'" he said, "Cosplay photography reverses this. The goal is to focus on the costume, expand the details, and turn the subject into 'somebody else.' It's an interesting genre of image-making."

Hughes said that what tends to set cosplay photography apart is the fact that it becomes a lot more multi-disciplinary than other forms of photography.

"Cosplay photography at its most basic is an interesting blend of model photography and commercial photography: you are marketing both the cosplayer and their costume. A good, standard photography shot will capture the cosplayer at a flattering angle and showcase the entire costume; the photo will be sharp, have nice bokeh, and follow good composition rules," Hughes said. "However, the best cosplay photography goes well beyond that, because cosplay isn't just about the model and the costume - it's about the character the model is dressed as. It's

about the series the character is from. Therefore, truly iconic cosplay photos will feature not just excellent composition, but interesting composition. Post-production editing recreates the atmosphere of the original series. Capturing the cosplayers doing in-character poses or having in-character interactions is key.

"An excellent cosplay photographer is a jack-of-all trades who can do scenery photography, model photography, journalistic photography, commercial photography, and on top of all that is a stage director for amateur models/actors, understands composition and their equipment well, and is a Photoshop master," she continued. "I don't know how much of that is required by other forms of photography, but it's no small feat!"

Besides needing to learn how to use a camera in different ways, plus knowing their way around some post-production editing software, there are plenty of other challenges that present themselves to the aspiring cosplay photographer. For one, the convention venue itself can be an issue, as cons are often loud, crowded, and held in poorly-lit hotels, exhibit halls, and even museums. McFadden recommended that photographers scout out locations around the convention venue

Photo credit: Kacie Doran

Photo credit: Kacie Doran

that don't look "jarring" when compared to the cosplayer – an armored knight is going to look pretty out of place in a hotel lobby, so it's important to make sure that, when shooting, there are desirable locations available in the area.

Of course, cosplay photography involves more than just one party – it requires there to be people on both sides of the camera. Frequently, photographers work with cosplayers that they've never met before that day, and it can be tricky to establish a good

Photo credit:
Archie Brown

relationship in a short amount of time.

"A photographer is frequently working with what amounts to amateur models. Most cosplayers don't have a good idea of what they look like from behind the camera lens, or know much about posing," Hughes said. "When working with strangers, the photographer must work to create a bridge of trust between themselves and the cosplayers, to help them pose and emote and feel relaxed in front of the camera. Photographers who achieve this frequently end up with the best photos."

Sometimes the biggest difficulties in the cosplay and photography communities arise when their interaction with each other is supposed to produce a monetary value of some sort. The economics of cosplay photography might be one of the most highly debated issues in the convention scene today.

"[One of the biggest issues is] the underestimation of a photographer's value and the judgement that comes with wanting to charge for your work," Doran said. "Putting your work out there is a huge feat in itself, and there are different opinions throughout the community on who should charge and who shouldn't, or if anyone should charge at all. At the end of the day it's up to the individual on what their work is worth."

But for the aspiring con photographer, it's generally not too hard to get started.

"Getting into cosplay photography isn't hard: all you need is a camera and the bravery to walk up to strangers and ask to take their photo," Hughes said. "But to be 'taken seriously,' I suppose, to have some name recognition or street cred, I'd guess you'd need a brand name or studio name, a website - even a Flickr account would work - and probably a DSLR, so it would take a little capital to get started and enough free time to regularly get photos up for consumption. And that takes a lot of dedication and hard work!"

And once the proper equipment is bought, it might not be a bad idea to hit up some buds before taking to the convention floor to get a good feel of how a photoshoot should go.

"I imagine it's easier to 'break in' if you have already been photographing weddings, events, or studied the subject in school," McFadden said. "Therefore, I think the best way to start the journey is to offer to take photos of your friends. They are the most understanding, the most flexible, and are great guinea pigs for your creative experimentation."

And once the first step is taken, it's important to keep going.

"Cosplay is firmly a hobby where you get out what you put in, and there's no such thing as wasted effort," Brown said, "If you go the extra mile, in any aspect of your costume or your photos, it'll show. And people will appreciate it!"

Photo credit: Archie Brown

Photographer Spotlight:
Archie Brown

What are the biggest challenges that a cosplay photographer tends to face?
Archie Brown (AB): In my experience, cosplay photography is much like any other profession, in that the part you are actually seen as "doing" is the easy bit. Finding the location, posing the subject, adjusting light, taking the photos, presents little difficulty, and is fun to boot. What makes cosplay photography in particular a challenge is the aspect of managing your online presence. Cosplay is linked with social media on virtually every level, and so to stay on the radar you need to have good word of mouth, an easily trackable and regularly updated portfolio, and a recognizable brand. This in effect makes you into a creative entrepreneur as a cosplay photographer, even if all you ever wanted to do is take pretty pictures of your friends.

You also do videos, which have become pretty popular recently. How are you able to make your videography stand out from the pack?
AB: Making videos that stand out from the trend is like shooting fish in a barrel. I apply common-sense principles like shooting variety, showing diversity, and producing videos that are more about the cosplayers themselves than whatever BS song was stuck in my head that day!

Would you say there are trends in cosplay photography in the same sense that there are noticeable trends in cosplay itself?
AB: There are plenty, but there are two noticeable trends in particular in the cosplay photography scene I hate the most. First is that derivative shot of a two-to-six person group all laying down on the ground with their heads together and their eyes closed. Also I'm bored to death of the current fad of repetitive, slapdash-edited generic dance-music cosplay music videos taken with a cheap steadicam that the photographer doesn't know how to use.

As someone who both acts as a photographer and as a cosplayer at conventions, how are you able to find a balance between the two at cons?
AB: As a cosplayer and a photographer, I more often than not have to sacrifice one for the other. And if I manage to pull off both at a con, then I don't have time to hang out with anybody.

Cosplayers Spotlight: Joker's Revenge

MOANA MCADAMS III
KALAMAOKLANI
"KALI"

JOHN MCADAMS III
NURI K.
"LORD JOKER"

ELISHA SIMMONS
AZRIEL ARRAKIS
"LADY RED"

ZAKIA CORRIA
ZALTANA KASHMIR

Please introduce yourself!
Nuri K. Amen Ra: I'm the owner of Burning Spear Comix and the creator and author of *The Wild Card Chronicles* comic book series. By day I'm a federal firearms dealer and the Pack Alpha, or leader, of the Joker's Revenge Motorcycle Family, who are also featured in the *WCC* comic.

What was your first introduction to the cosplay hobby? What was it about cosplay that made you want to participate?
Nuri K.: Our first encounter with cosplay was at the Baltimore Comic-Con in 2014. We saw some of the most awe-inspiring costume designs we had ever seen. While we were there in the midst of it all, we noticed many cosplayers taking notice of us and our unique look. To the attendees, we were something new and different, which surprised us because we were simply dressed as ourselves in our MC colors and shields. So at the next comic-con we attended we really stepped it up and took it to the next level by incorporating the face paint. Things really took off for us after that.

What is your approach to cosplay?
Nuri K.: We're cosplayers who are actually dressed up as ourselves – this is who we are. Each one of us is a character within the *WCC* universe. Having the ability to dress up as your own super hero is an amazing feeling! Costume production is easy for us, because the most vital parts of our costumes – the motorcycle vest and the shield/badge – are our actual official club colors that we wear when we ride. The face makeup that we wear is done for us by our makeup artist, Chavon Williams.

What kind of issues do you feel cosplayers face the most these days?
Nuri K.: The greatest issue cosplayers face, in my opinion, is the lack of evolution from the old-school comic book vendors. These guys must come to understand that it's the advent of the cosplay scene that brings their comic books to life and, in effect, aids comic book sales in a big way. Seeing the cosplayers makes us want to buy the comic and read what the character is all about.

Anything else you'd like to add?
Nuri K.: Burning Spear Comix and *The Wild Card Chronicles* universe is unique because it mixes a comic book with actual cosplay. Our flagship series illustrates the tales of real-life bikers and is also written by actual bikers. These stories are then set against a backdrop of urban legends and mythology to bring our readers a tale like no other. You can find out all about us at burningspearcomix.com!

Rainy Day Projects For Kids

Fleece Hat

If you have a kid who's interested in cosplay, it's never too soon to get them started on some simple projects where they can practice their sewing skills. But as much as they might want to, kids typically don't start out making full suits of high-tech armor. This simple hat pattern will get them some experience in sewing, plus will potentially provide some costume items, depending on how you use it. Fleece and felt are some of the best materials for simple projects, because they are thick, soft, and best of all, they don't fray, so you won't need to do any extra hemming or serging if you don't want to. We of course recommend parental supervision for a project that involves this much sewing.

Materials:

- Fleece
- Scissors
- Sewing machine (or needle and thread if you're hand-sewing)
- Straight pins
- Measuring tape

Step 1:

Measure the head circumference of the person who will be wearing the finished product with your measuring tape. Divide that number by four, and then add about an inch to the divided number. Write this number down – this will be your panel width.

Step 2:

Lay your fleece out flat and cut out four panels. They should look like the image here – sort of a rounded triangle shape. Make sure they are as wide as the number you reached in step 1. You can cut them out on the fold of the fabric to save some time and sewing later, if you want.

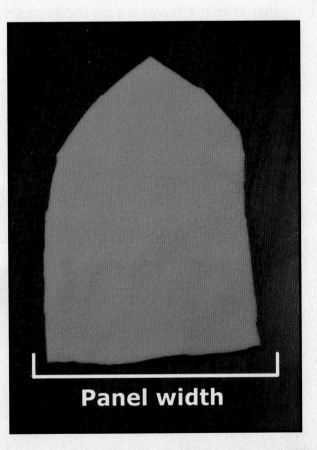

Panel width

Step 3: Lay two panels on top of each other, and pin up one side. Sew them together. For the sake of this tutorial, we're using a machine, but you can use this as an opportunity to practice hand-sewing as well. We're also using a different colored thread than the fabric so that you can see it clearly in the photos, but you probably want to have matching thread to your fabric.

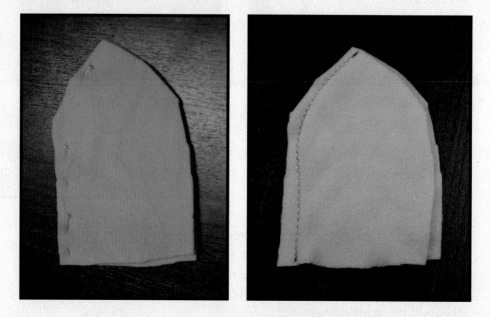

Step 4: Repeat this process with the other panels, while making sure that all of the seams are on the same side – you don't want any raw edges to be on the outside of the hat. But if you mess it up a little, having a seam-ripper on hand is always a good thing.

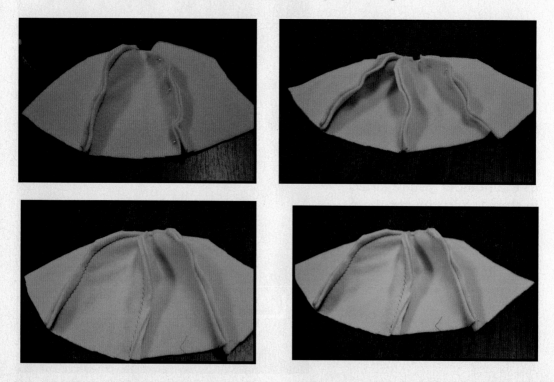

Step 5: When everything is put together, it should look something like this. At this point, you should flip it inside out and try it on. It should be snug but not too tight. If it is too loose (if it's sliding around on top of your head) you can go back and take in the seams ever so slightly on each side so that it fits better. Be sure to snip off any loose threads.

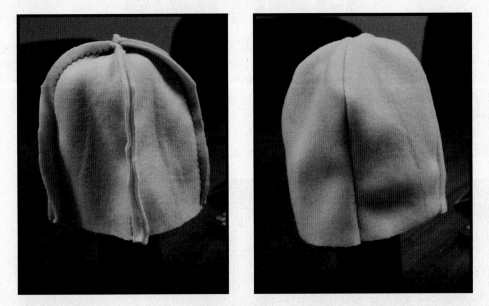

Step 6: At this point, you can do a number of different things. The most basic thing to do is to simply hem the bottom of it so that it's clean, rather than having the raw edge at the bottom. But you can also add designs from your favorite series, either by gluing them on or sewing them on, to create a unique piece of headgear. Another idea for this pattern is to make the panels significantly taller than they need to be, so that you can pull it down over the top half of your face – by cutting out eyeholes, now you have a unique hero mask perfect for lots of costumes!

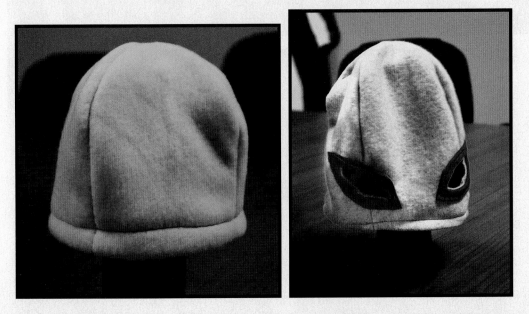

Rainy Day Projects

Craft Foam

Craft foam is a great material for kids to use because it is soft and spongy as well as being incredibly versatile. The thin sheets come in a huge variety of colors and are generally super inexpensive – it's become a great alternative material for even a lot of experienced cosplayers who are looking for a way to keep their budget low on props.

For kids though, craft foam makes for some easy and fun rainy day projects that can even lead to some head-starts on their first cosplays.

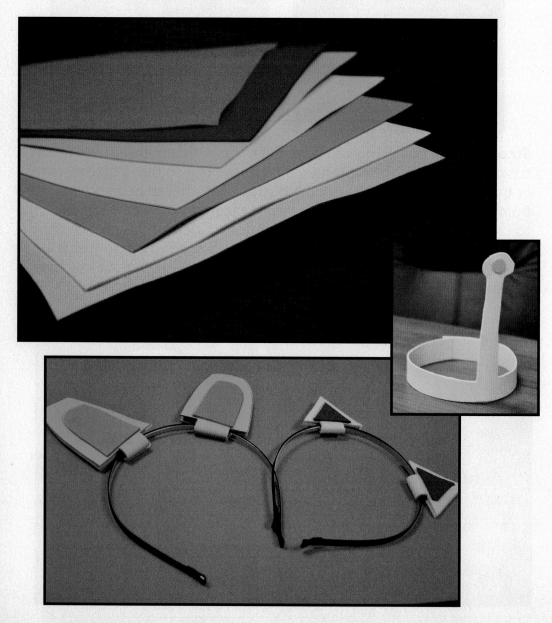

Masks

Requires: Foam sheet, elastic

Step 1: Start by taking a sheet of whatever color craft foam you're using and folding it in half. Then, using the fold as the guide to where the bridge of your nose will be, cut out the shape of the mask.

Step 2: Unfold the shape and hold it up to your face, then trim the mask piece if it is too large for your needs. It might be a good idea to mark where your eyes land on the mask so that you can cut out eyeholes in a more accurate fashion.

Step 3: Re-fold the piece and then fold it again to make the initial cut for the eyeholes. Then, finish snipping out the eyeholes.

Step 4: When you open it up, it should look something like this. The most common means of finishing this up is by attaching an elastic band to either side to wrap around the back of the head, but do whatever works for you!

 # Character/animal ears

Requires: Foam sheets, headband, glue

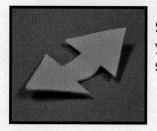 **Step 1:** Cut out two fairly small pieces of foam. They should be rectangular and as close to the same size as possible.

Step 2: Fold one of the pieces in half, and make two small cuts about a third of the way in from either side. Then cut off the outer thirds, leaving the middle one intact. This will serve as the loop that you will stick your headband through, so make sure it will be wide enough for the band you intend to use.

Step 3: While still folded, cut out the shape you want the ears to be. Repeat this for the second ear.

Step 4: If you want, add a second (or third, fourth, whatever!) to the piece to act as an inside color or whatever else you want.

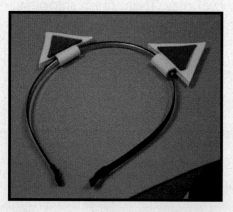 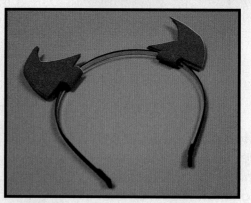

Step 5: Glue the inside of the ears together, making sure not to glue the loop shut, then thread the headband through the loops. Now you've got a headband that can work as an easy cosplay accessory! Try using the same technique for things like different animal ears, horns, a crown, or whatever else you might need!

Crowns

Requires: Foam sheets, potentially sticky Velcro

Step 1: Get a large foam sheet in the color you need and fold it in half.

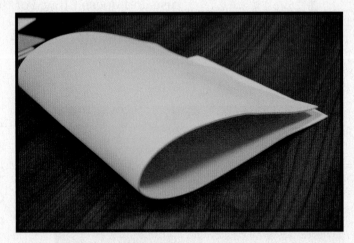

Step 2: Using the center as the point of reference for the front of the crown, cut out the shape you need.

Step 3: If it's already the right size for the head in question, you can just glue the pieces together in the back, but if it may need some adjustment, it might be smart to stick some Velcro on there as the means of staying together.

Step 4: Accessorize with other foam colors as necessary!

As we mentioned, fleece is a really good material for the youngest crafters due to the fact that it is easy to use and doesn't fray. For the little heroes who need a cape to accompany their costume, here's a super easy way for them to make it themselves!

Materials:

- Fleece (about a yard)
- Scissors
- Glue or a sewing machine
- Felt sheets or extra fleece colors
- Marker

Step 1: Lay your fleece out on a flat surface and, at about two or three inches from the edge, draw a line starting from the fold for how wide you want the top of the cape to be. Remember – you are starting on the fold, so it should be half as much as the end result.

Step 2: Draw a line from the end of the cape top that angles out to the bottom of the fabric.

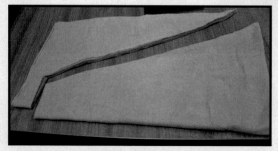

Step 3: Cut out the shape you just made and put it aside.

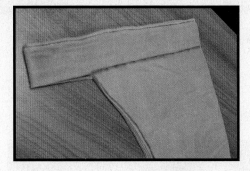

Step 4: Using the leftover fabric, cut out the strip of fabric at the top. Draw a line to guide you if you need to. This will be your tie for the cape.

Step 5: Unfold the cape and lay it out flat. Then unfold the tie piece and center it on the cape. Using either strong glue or your sewing machine, attach the tie to the top of the cape.

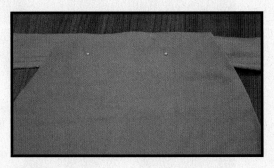

Step 6: Turn it over (to the "fashion side") and now you have a blank canvas on which to work. If you're trying to re-create a famous design, center it on the back. But otherwise, go nuts! You can sew or glue your design onto the back – because of the amount of angles in our design here, we went ahead and glued it.

Now you have a functional and comfortable hero cape! Whether you're wearing it to the next comic show or just around the house for make-believe, this is a simple and fun craft project, no matter how big you are!

Cosplayer Spotlight:
— Lisa Tran —

How did you get started in cosplay?

I didn't know what cosplay was when I made my first costume. By that time in my life, I'd been going to SDCC for several years and of course had noticed people dressing up in costume and just thought it looked like amazing fun. I had an irresistible urge to dress as Psylocke, my favorite member of the X-Men, so I made my first costume by hand. After all, who wouldn't want to dress up as a superhero?

We heard about you from Billy Tucci, the creator of Shi, a character you're known for cosplaying. What are some of the different versions of Shi you've done?

I love the beautiful and very fierce look of Shi! I've made two versions of her - the famous red outfit and the 20th anniversary edition kimono. I saw the 20th anniversary version a week before SDCC so I had to really push myself to make it. There are still some parts of it I would still like to perfect.

What was Billy's reaction the first time he saw you as his character?

Billy is wonderful and was very welcoming when I first met him in full Shi costume! I was very nervous meeting him but he is truly a creator who appreciates his fans so I had a fantastic time speaking with him.

What other characters have you done?

I have cosplayed as other comic characters but I've also made costumes from video games and anime. A couple of my favorites are Juclecia from the video game *Magna Carta* and Seung Mina from the video game *Soul Calibur*. And of course Psylocke, my original costume!

What memorable personal experiences do you associate with cosplay?

I've met many wonderful people through cosplaying. It's very satisfying to be able to connect with others through a shared love of gaming or reading. Cosplayers are dreamers who like to live their fantasies out in the real world every once in awhile. I love that.

Do you generally make your own costumes, have others make them, or purchase them?

With the exception of one costume, I've always made my own. The one time I decided to have someone else help me, I wasn't quite satisfied with the end product and had to remake quite a bit of it. I have on occasion purchased a shirt or an accessory to complete a costume, however, and I had the weapon for my Seung Mina costume commissioned.

What sorts of reactions have you heard about your costumes?

All very positive!

What do you think cosplay adds to the convention-going experience?

Quite a bit, actually! It's something that con goers look forward to as good people watching. On a deeper level, it shows you that you aren't alone - there are clearly people around you who love the same things that you do and show that love proudly by dressing like characters from their favorite movies/comics/video games.

What challenges or issues do you think cosplayers face the most?

I don't agree with the idea that a person needs to resemble the character they want to portray. If someone feels a connection to a character or likes their design, that's all that matters. I wish we weren't judged by how much we resemble a character or how we don't or how old we are or how we aren't the right ethnicity.

What issues, if any, have you faced because of cosplay?

Cosplay is something I do just once a year so it doesn't have a negative impact on my life.

What developments in cosplay would you like to see?

I like that cosplay has developed into a hobby that is pretty accessible to everyone now. You can find a lot of available costumes online or commission things that are harder to find. It's open to everyone regardless of sewing skill. If someone has been thinking of cosplaying, I say, don't think about it - just do it!

Photographer Spotlight:
Kacie Doran

What did you have an interest in first – photography or cosplay?

Kacie Doran (KD): Probably a little surprising since I feel like most people get into cosplay first, but I was first into photography! I had my camera for about two years before I even got into cosplay.

What piqued your interest in photography?

KD: I wanted to document things in the way that I saw them. I think everyone sees the world differently, we choose what we want to see and what we don't, and there's a million angles that you could look at something from. I just wanted to tell what I saw in those things.

What do you think differs between cosplay photography and other more "conventional" forms of photography?

KD: Personally, it's the telling of a story instead of the capture of a moment. It's translating the series into something that could look like a still from a live action production of it. I think photography in every way is documentary, but it's how you present that documentation that makes it so different from editorial photography or wedding photography.

What are the biggest challenges that a cosplay photographer tends to face?

KD: The underestimation of a photographer's value and the judgement that comes with wanting to charge for your work. Putting your work out there is a huge feat in itself, and there are different opinions throughout the community on who should charge and who shouldn't, or if anyone should charge at all. At the end of the day it's up to the individual on what their work is worth.

Also night shoots. Better have your light equipment ready kiddos, because your camera is gonna hate you.

Would you say there are trends in cosplay photography in the same sense that there are noticeable trends in cosplay itself?

KD: Hmm, not so much trends, I'd say that it's more common to see individual styles. Everyone has a different shooting style, a different editing style, favorite equipment that they like to shoot with, etc. I think that changes with the waves of different equipment and editing software that emerge from year to year, but I don't think there are any specified trends that happen in the photography end of the community as much as the cosplay end of it, such as series that EVERYONE AND YOUR MOTHER are into.

Cosplayer Spotlight: Zach Bravo

What first got you interested in cosplay?

Zach Bravo (ZB): Before cosplay was in my vocabulary, I was just a huge fan of Spider-Man and I always wanted an authentic Spider-Man costume. I was about 15 years old at the time and all I could ever think about was just getting my hands on those red and blue tights. Once I received it, I couldn't stop wearing it. I would literally walk around the house in the costume like it was nobody's business. I would see videos on YouTube of other people in Spider-Man costumes and they would do kids parties and I thought to myself, "Man, I would love to see kids reactions if they saw me in my Spider-Man costume at their party."

But then my step-father told me about this convention where they have booths and panels full of awesome stuff that had to deal with comic books, superheroes, etc. So when I attended New York Comic Con in the fall of 2010, I was just amazed and saw all the cool things over there. I especially saw people in costume. And all I remember was these well fabricated costumes. They were brought to life! So the next year, I had went to the 2011 convention and I wore my Spider-Man costume and I was given so much recognition. That was a fun year, and also a year when I gained my interest in cosplay.

What's been one of your best or most memorable experiences in cosplay?

ZB: Whenever I go to a convention, I am always having a blast. But something special happened one time when I was in my red and blues. After the "paparazzi" were taking my photos, all I can see was a line of kids just dying to see me! Some were jumping up and down full of excitement, some were hiding behind their parents, but there was this line full of kids. At first I was like, "Oh no! I'm gonna get attacked!" Thankfully that didn't happen.

These two kids came up to me and had given me their Spider-Man comic books. I thought they were giving it to me as a gift. Unfortunately that wasn't the case, they wanted me to sign their comic book, as Spider-Man of course. So I signed their comics and I took pictures with them. There was another kid that literally grabbed my hand and asked me to go hang out with him. I guess he wanted Spidey all to himself. Basically, these are the best moments when it comes to kids. I once shot some "webs" at a kid and he got so excited he gave me a huge hug. Cosplaying to me is like being a character at Disney World...but kinda not...but you get what I mean!

What challenges or issues do you think cosplayers face the most?

ZB: A struggle that some cosplayers go through are other people's opinions. You know the type of person that just critiques just about everything? Yeah, that type of person. Some people who are in costume, whether they are accurate or not accurate to a character, should still be appreciated by the fact someone is even bringing the character to life! And the fact that some are downgraded for not having an accurate costume is a totally not okay!

Cosplay is another way to let you be you, just how dancers are, just how rock stars are. It should not be hidden. Cosplay to me is sort of a gateway to exit reality without exiting reality. It's a fun hobby and nobody should be given any slice of discrimination for that! There are cosplayers, people to be precise, out there who are self-conscious about themselves. And that is the reason of people who want to be critics and feel good about themselves. Cosplay should be nothing more than a having a good time and being happy. We are in the 21st century here: support yourself and support everyone else. Just because something is not accurate to your eyes, doesn't mean that it's not to theirs.

Cosplayer Spotlight:
FenixEmber Cosplay

Please introduce yourself!
FenixEmber Cosplay (FEC): Hey hey! My name's Allison or Ember of FenixEmber Cosplay (trying to get that name to stick—it's totally weird). I'm 24 and I'm from Long Island, NY. My occupation is Batgirl… no I'm totally kidding. I definitely have a real, grown up job.

What challenges or issues do you think cosplayers face the most?
FEC: So much. There's a lot of drama in the cosplay community. It's such a competitive environment sometimes and it doesn't need to be. People forget it's supposed to be fun, and I think a lot of that comes from the fact there are the lucky few that get to do this for a living. I do have to say though, I think most of the drama comes from people on the outside. Since I've joined up with the DC Cosplayers East group, they've been nothing but supportive. We all look out for each

other and help when we can.

Besides that, there's everything with body image, and people being critical of how you made your costume, etc. Again, it's mostly outside people that don't understand and are more fans of cosplayers, but it still sucks. But having friends that will back you up alleviates a lot of those issues.

Any other cosplay thoughts you'd like to share?
FEC: Cosplay should totally 100 million percent be about having fun and doing what you love. Yeah, it's basically taken over my life in the way that I'm always adding costumes to my list and spending my free time researching, designing/building, and buying stuff for a cosplay but it still makes me happy. Don't let anyone tell you it's weird and just be yourself. And I totally can't say this enough—have fun!!

EVERYONE DESERVES A
GOLDEN AGE

GIVE BACK TO THE CREATORS WHO GAVE YOU YOUR DREAMS.